To Well
Family
In Love & Light
Rev. Louise Michaud

A Daughter's Journey

A Spirit from Heaven

Louise Michaud

BALBOA.
PRESS

A DIVISION OF HAY HOUSE

Balboa Press books may be ordered through booksellers or by contacting:

Balboa Press
A Division of Hay House
1663 Liberty Drive
Bloomington, IN 47403
www.balboapress.com
1 (877) 407-4847

Because of the dynamic nature of the Internet, any web addresses or
links contained in this book may have changed since publication and
may no longer be valid. The views expressed in this work are solely those
of the author and do not necessarily reflect the views of the publisher,
and the publisher hereby disclaims any responsibility for them.

The author of this book does not dispense medical advice or prescribe the use
of any technique as a form of treatment for physical, emotional, or medical
problems without the advice of a physician, either directly or indirectly. The
intent of the author is only to offer information of a general nature to help
you in your quest for emotional and spiritual well-being. In the event you use
any of the information in this book for yourself, which is your constitutional
right, the author and the publisher assume no responsibility for your actions.

Any people depicted in stock imagery provided by Thinkstock are
models, and such images are being used for illustrative purposes only.
Certain stock imagery © Thinkstock.

Printed in the United States of America.

ISBN: 978-1-4525-2082-7 (sc)
ISBN: 978-1-4525-2084-1 (hc)
ISBN: 978-1-4525-2083-4 (e)

Library of Congress Control Number: 2014915164

Balboa Press rev. date: 8/26/2014

Dedication

I dedicate this book to my beautiful daughter, Chantal.
If it were not for you,
this book would never have been written.
I thank you for your love, support, and understanding.
You were an inspiration to many people throughout your
lifetime,
and you continue to inspire me from the other side.
I am so proud you chose me to be your mother.
I love you, miss you, and am so grateful
that we shared this lifetime together.

Contents

Author's Note

A *Daughter's Journey* was written during the most difficult time in my life, grieving the loss of my beautiful daughter, Chantal, who passed away on July 22, 2012. She inspired many people throughout her lifetime, including me. Her inspiration has given me strength and has compelled me to share her story with the world. She lived each day to the fullest, while she battled cancer and heart disease from her earliest years.

Here, I talk about her fears, anxieties, and frustrations. The love and compassion, the patience and understanding she felt for other people made her who she truly was, a loving spirit. I share her story in the hope of helping families whose lives have been affected by illness or are grieving the loss of a child.

We all grieve in a different way. I speak from my heart when I say that knowing that my daughter is around me and communicates with me has helped my grieving her loss. I know that death is not final. Her soul lives on. It is a new beginning, and I am so grateful to be a part of her journey.

Acknowledgements

This book is written with specials thanks to the following people, who were a big part of Chantal's life.

First of all, I thank my beautiful daughter Chantal, for it is your journey, your courage, and your inspiration that has led me to write this book. You touched the lives of many people, and you continue to inspire on the other side. I love you with all my heart, miss you, and look forward to the day we meet again.

I am so grateful to God, my angels, and my guides for giving me the guidance, the courage, and the confidence to share my daughter's journey with the world.

Alain Fortier, my wonderful husband, thank you for all the love, support, and encouragement you have given me over the years; for loving, caring, and taking my children into your heart, making them a part of your life; and for always being there for us. I am so grateful you came into our lives.

John Commerford, her dad, I thank you for the two beautiful children we had together and for sharing those memories for twenty-two years. I am grateful that we remain friends after everything we experienced together.

Thomas Commerford, my son, I love you and thank you for being her brother. Thank you for loving her and for helping care for her during those difficult years. I realize there were times when it was tough for you, and you never complained. Know that she loved you and that she always looked up to you as her big brother.

Adam Barrington, I thank you for loving my daughter, caring for her, and supporting her the way you did. Thank you for remaining by her side throughout this whole ordeal and, most of all, for helping my daughter to experience being in a loving relationship. I am so grateful to you.

Alissa Cassidy, I thank you for being such a good friend to Chantal, for supporting her and encouraging her when she needed it most. You were her sounding board when she was down, and you knew exactly how to boost her morale. You were there with her when we couldn't be, and for that I am grateful to you. You were a true friend, and I know Chantal loved you and cherished your friendship.

Shelley Tatum, Chantal's nurse and her friend, I thank you for allowing Chantal into your heart and being such a good friend to me and especially to her. The love and compassion that you gave my daughter will never be forgotten. Your friendship meant the world to her.

Jennifer Ohrling, I thank you for being her dear friend and companion. You were like a big sister to Chantal. You shared wonderful memories together at camp and on a personal level. Being bridesmaid in your wedding made her feel very special. You came into her life when she was little and were able to see her grow into a beautiful young lady. I am so grateful you shared all those years together.

Jeremy Kostal, her living angel, I can't thank you enough for saving my daughter's life, for never leaving her side and bringing her home to us. You are a wonderful being, and I will never, ever forget you. Chantal loved you and thought the world of you, as do I. Thank you for being such a wonderful friend to Chantal.

Anita Pizycki, my friend and my mentor, there is a reason you came into my life, and knowing you has changed my life forever. I have learned a lot from you, and I cherish our friendship. I can't thank you enough for making Chantal's memorial service the wonderful memory I will never forget.

Cathy Timmins, Chantal's friend and my friend, you were a big part of Chantal's life. You always made her feel special. She trusted you and felt comfortable confiding in you. I am truly grateful that you were there for her when I couldn't be. She loved you, as I love you. Thank you for being there for her.

Val Green, my good friend, we shared some wonderful times together. We spent many nights comforting each other, and supporting each other through the good times and the bad. We liked to do the same things and enjoyed each other's company. You were there when I was at my lowest, and for that I am truly grateful.

Special thanks goes to my family: my brother Michel, his wife Nicole, and their family; my sister Ginette (Chantal's godmother), her husband Sandy, and their family; and my late sister Carolle, her husband Tom, and their family. She loved every one of you so much. Thank you for being a part of her life and making wonderful memories together. I would also like to thank all of Alain's family for making Chantal feel like she was a member of their family.

And for all the people who were a part of Chantal's life whose names I did not mention, I thank you and am truly grateful to every one of you.

Introduction

E ver since I was six years old, I felt a strong connection with God. I couldn't explain it at that age. I just felt the connection and knew it was right. I will admit there were certain things that I questioned when it came to our religious beliefs. One of the questions that bothered me the most was, "How can a loving God punish me for sinning? What could I have possibly done at that age that would merit me being punished by a loving God?" This truly puzzled me. I never believed it. I could not understand this. I asked my parents and teachers that exact question. My dad would simply say, "You need to go to church and be a good Catholic." My teachers would look at me as if to say, "How can you ask such a question? Just sit there and be quiet." I was never happy or satisfied. So, I simply stopped asking.

As a teenager I started to have what we call "gut feelings" about certain things in my life and the people around me. I guess I always had this intuitive gift but became more aware of those feelings as I grew older. At that time, I did not always act on it, because I had no idea what they were, other than "gut feelings." Sometimes my thoughts and feelings would manifest into reality.

For example, during my school years there were certain kids I would meet for the first time. I would feel a very negative energy around their presence. This gave me a very uncomfortable feeling, and I knew I did not want to be around them. I also recall an occasion when my husband and I were out driving a feeling of fear came over me. I felt the car in front of us was going to come straight at us and hit us. That was exactly what happened.

Unfortunately, it wasn't until my forties that some of these experiences caused me to want to search for answers, to seek understanding, and to pray to God for guidance. I knew then I had to stop seeking answers from the physical world. I needed to put all my trust and faith in God and the spiritual world. Through prayers, God made me realize I needed to make positive changes in my life for me to be able to understand what I was feeling. I had made wrong choices and mistakes throughout my life. I knew now that for my life to improve I would need to make those changes. There were other answers that did not come to me as quickly as I had hoped. It was then I understood that first I needed to make these changes, before I was to receive the guidance that would change my life forever.

Sometimes we pray for solutions or guidance, and we feel that our prayers are not answered. You ask why? It is not that our prayers are being ignored. God knows what our plans are. He will put forward everything to help us achieve a goal. First, we need to make changes to receive what we asked for. God will not hand our desires to us on a silver platter. We need to do some of the legwork ourselves.

You could say that knowing these changes was another answer to a prayer. I started to meditate, read self-help books, attend workshops, and listen to inspirational tapes. I enrolled in a two-year program at a spiritual school, became an ordained spiritualist minister, developed my psychic abilities, and learned different hands-on healing techniques, which I was able to perform on my daughter after her stroke. All of these wonderful tools helped me to get started on making positive changes in my life.

Great things have happened to me because of all these changes. The first was learning to love and forgive myself. Second was learning to love and forgive those who hurt me. I learnt to be more patient and more compassionate, and to see good in everyone. But most of all, I found the courage to write this book during the most difficult time in my life, grieving the loss of my daughter. The love and inspiration I felt I received from Chantal from the other side gave me the motivation to share her journey with the world. I truly believe that her story will touch the hearts of many people and that her legacy will live on.

CHAPTER 1

An Unexpected Arrival

I t was the summer of 1967 and our last day at school. To celebrate our graduation, our class decided to have a beach party at Sherkston Beach that weekend. We also thought it would be more fun if we invited some outside friends to join us that day. I set my alarm to wake up at seven o'clock that morning so I would have plenty of time to have everything ready before my ride came to pick me up.

I woke up to a beautiful sunny Saturday morning. The weather forecast had predicted the weather to be in the nineties. I packed my cooler with plenty of food and drinks for the day. We arrived at the beach around eleven. The sun was already beating down on us. We unpacked the car and put all our gear in place. The only way to cool off was to go for a swim. We all ran into the water. It was so cool and refreshing, especially after sweating so much during the ride there.

Our day was spent playing volleyball, water polo, and horseshoes and taking walks along the beach. You could feel the warm sand filtering through your toes. It was a great day filled with fun and laughter. To end this perfect day we all sat around a campfire and roasted marshmallows. While I was sitting there, I happened to notice this young man staring at me. He had dark hair, was good-looking, and appeared to be tall. I said to myself, *Did he just arrive, or has he been here all along and I just happened to notice him?* When he saw me staring at him, he got up and started to walk towards me. My heart started to beat really fast. I thought, *Oh, no! He is coming toward me. What will I say to him?* He didn't give me a chance to speak, as he immediately sat down beside me and introduced himself as John. I said, "Hello, my name is Louise. I'm happy to meet you." I asked him how he'd found out about the party. John told me he came with a friend and had only just arrived.

Within minutes I started to feel a little more relaxed. I found out John was an only child. He lived in my home town in St. Catharines. He was four years older than I and working as an industrial millwright. We talked for hours and got to know each other. By the end of the evening, John asked me if I would like to go out with him the following Saturday. I was really excited, as I was hoping he would ask me out. I said, "Yes, I would love to go out with you." What a wonderful way to end the school year.

I really looked forward to my date with John. Earlier that week we had talked about going to the movies. As soon as I saw the car pull in our driveway, I became very nervous. Even though I felt comfortable with John at the beach, I was still a bit anxious waiting for his arrival. We had a wonderful time that night and planned to go out again.

Having completed high school, I found employment as a receptionist for a law firm. John and I continued dating and got along very well. We enjoyed each other's company and we had a lot of things in common. After a year and a half of going out together, we decided to get married. On September 5, 1969, John and I became husband and wife. I was twenty years old at the time.

Two years into our marriage, John and I decided it was time to start a family. My beautiful son, Thomas, was born on March 21, 1971, weighing in at nine pounds and one ounce. He was the sweetest little boy, with dark hair, big fat rosy cheeks, and a wonderful appetite. I was so proud to be his mom, and John was so proud to have a son.

Thomas was a very good baby, which made it easier on me. The only thing I found difficult was that Thomas had his days and nights mixed up. He would sleep all day and be up all night. Being a stay-at-home mom gave me the opportunity to rest during the day while he slept. He had a tremendous appetite; I couldn't get the food into his mouth fast enough. Thomas learned to walk by the time he was nine months old and could speak clearly well before his third birthday. When Thomas turned five I enrolled him in kindergarten. He enjoyed school and made a lot of new friends. I decided it was time for me to go back to work.

John and I had talked about having another child, but the years flew by so quickly. Before we knew it, Thomas was twelve years old. He was growing up fast and doing very well in school. I was working at a small novelty shop and really enjoyed it. The thought of another child no longer occurred to us.

3

In the spring of 1982 I became pregnant with our second child. I was then thirty-three years old. The thought of having another child was emotionally overwhelming for me. I felt scared and dismayed that I would have to start all over again. I had given away all the things we needed for a new baby. I would have to buy everything. I would have to quit work. I would have to worry about getting babysitters. Some of these thoughts were silly, but even so, every one of them was overpowering at the time.

I really liked my job, and I wanted to continue working. When I found out I was pregnant, I knew it would change my life forever. Yet I believe things happen for a reason. After the initial shock of learning I was pregnant, I started thinking about the new creation inside of me, and this thought helped me find such peace and love that all of the earlier negative emotions disappeared.

My due date was early February, but my daughter was especially anxious to come into the world. She decided to arrive on November 27, 1982, the day before her dad's birthday. I went into labor on a Friday night, and Chantal was born at 5:27 a.m. Saturday morning. She was two months premature, weighing three pounds and three ounces and measuring eighteen inches. That is when our lives changed forever.

My daughter was very beautiful and very tiny. She was a fighter from the moment she took her first breath. The day after she was born, her weight slipped down to two pounds and fourteen ounces. While we were told that this was normal for a newborn, considering how little she was, the weight loss terrified us. The first time I saw Chantal in the incubator brought tears to my eyes. My first thought was, *Is this my fault? Did I cause this to happen to my baby? Maybe I did not eat right; could I have taken better care of myself?* I tried not to think that way, but once in a while those negative thoughts would pop into my head.

Seeing Chantal's frail little body just lie there with a feeding tube inserted in her nose was heart-wrenching. The fact that I could not hold her close to me, have her feel the love I had for her, was one of the hardest things I ever had to feel. Since I could not hold my daughter in my arms, I did get some comfort in putting my hand through a small opening in front of the incubator and hold her little hand. I talked to Chantal. I let her know how much I loved her, how much I longed to hold her and take her home with me. The doctor signed my discharge papers. It was time for me to leave the hospital. Having to go home and not being able to take Chantal with me was heartbreaking. I went back every day to be with my daughter. In the evening I would go back with my husband John and my son, Thomas. We always had a bet as to how much weight she had gained. Some days it was only a quarter of an ounce. Yet we never had any doubt that Chantal was going to get better, and every day she would improve.

I will never forget this. Chantal had been in the hospital four weeks already. It was a Friday morning, time for me to head to the hospital to see my baby. When I walked into the nursery, I screamed and started to cry. "Oh my God, I can hold my baby!" The day I was praying for had finally arrived. I was so happy.

The nurses were excited for me. They told me that since Chantal was getting stronger every day, she was able to be transferred to a nursery bed. I was so grateful to the staff and to God for taking care of my little girl. Finally, I could hold my sweet baby in my arms. What a comfort to hold her close to me for the first time. She was so small and so beautiful, I couldn't stop kissing her. There were times I was afraid I wasn't holding her the right way. It felt awkward but wonderful at the same time.

I could hold her for only a short period of time. Chantal needed all her strength, and holding her too long was tiresome. I wanted to call my husband at work and tell him the good news. I decided to keep the wonderful news quiet until we came back that evening to see our baby. I wanted them to be as surprised as I was. It was very difficult for me to keep silent. We finished supper, I quickly put the dishes in the dishwasher, and off we went to the hospital. I really wanted to see the expression on both their faces, so I let them go in first to the nursery. When they saw Chantal in the little bed, my son, with a big smile on his face, immediately ran to her bedside. The look of excitement on my husband's face made me cry. They were both so happy they too could hold her now. In the days to follow, John and Thomas would run into the nursery to see who could hold her first. Since I was able to have that wonderful opportunity during the day, I let them.

Every day Chantal was getting stronger, I couldn't wait to get to the hospital to see how much she had progressed overnight. We prayed for the day Chantal would come home where she belonged. During the time Chantal was in the hospital, only a few family members were allowed to see her at a time, and only through a glass window. Chantal's aunts, uncles, nieces, and nephews were also looking forward to that special day. Two weeks later our prayers were answered. Chantal was released from the hospital, weighing five pounds four ounces.

We were incredibly excited taking her home. As parents we were also very proud of how much Chantal had progressed in the last six weeks. We had her room all ready for her arrival. When we got home our golden retriever, Tara, was right there beside us, wondering who this little person was. Tara was a very gentle dog, so we knew not to fear her being around Chantal. I put Chantal down in a cradle I had borrowed. Even in there she looked so tiny. She did not occupy much space. It would be a while before she could sleep in her own crib.

I watched her as she slept. I couldn't keep my eyes off her. She was so beautiful. She was perfect. Her skin was a beautiful shade of rose. Her hair was dark and silky. Her eyes were a lovely shade of dark blue, almost navy. In the beginning I found I was a little nervous having to bathe her and change her. It had been twelve years since Thomas was born, and because Chantal was so little I was a bit apprehensive.

As a "preemie," Chantal was able to eat only two ounces of milk at a time. My days of sleeping through the night were over. She would wake me up every two hours. As soon as I put her back to bed and started to doze off, it was time to get up again for her next feeding. It did not take long before I was able to increase her milk to four ounces. Shortly after that I was able to increase it to six ounces. This allowed her to sleep a little longer. At the age of six months, Chantal weighed ten pounds twelve ounces and was sleeping through the night. I was very grateful that I could now get a good night's sleep, but most of all, that she was doing so well. It didn't take long before she was eating solid food.

Thomas was really proud of his baby sister. He helped us when it came time for her feeding; and without complaining, he would babysit for us whenever we needed to go out. He was her big brother and wanted to take care of her. Along with her brother, our golden retriever, Tara, watched over her. The dog would lie down beside her crib whenever Chantal went to sleep. When Chantal started to walk, the dog would forever follow her throughout the house. Even though Tara was Thomas's dog, she and Chantal became real good buddies.

I was told by a nurse that because Chantal was two months premature, she would be slower in her development. Happily, that was not the case for my daughter. Chantal still had a great appetite. Her weight was increasing slowly but steadily. Chantal started forming words. Her first word was *Dadda*. John was so proud. I knew I was never going to live that one down, but I was happy for him. In June 1983, at the age of seven months, she turned over for the first time. She also developed a very hearty laugh when you made faces at her. By August, Chantal was able to sit up without any assistance.

One time when I put Chantal on a blanket on the floor in the living room, I left for a minute to get something from the next room, and when I turned to go back into the living room, she was right there by my feet. I screamed! I did not expect her to be there. The scream scared Chantal and made her cry. I immediately picked her up to console her. "Oh, sweetie. Mommy did not mean to scare you. I am so sorry. Mommy loves you so much." I held her tight, gave her a big hug and a kiss. I was so excited for both of us. I couldn't wait to tell John and Thomas that Chantal was now able to crawl.

In early December she was able to stand on her own, and by the middle of December she walked for the first time. My husband and I were sitting in the living room watching television, and Thomas was in his room. Chantal was sitting on the floor playing with one of her toys. The next thing we knew, Chantal was crawling towards the coffee table. She stood up, balanced herself, and started to walk. We called Thomas to come right away. We watched to see what she was going to do next. She turned herself around and started to walk towards us. "Chantal's walking," John said in amazement. It was a very proud moment for all of us. She was thirteen months old.

Chantal was progressing normally. She was forming more words. Her vocabulary was increasing. I had returned to work full-time, so I needed a sitter during the day. I had interviewed a few girls. One in particular that I felt comfortable with, and Chantal took a shine to her, so I hired her. For the next three years she took very good care of my daughter. I never regretted my choice. I was very grateful to her.

In September, just before Chantal's fourth birthday, John and I had decided to enroll her in prekindergarten. We felt she needed some form of normality in her life. It was only three days a week, half days. Being around other children would be good for Chantal. She loved school and playing with the other kids. She made a lot of friends. It was a good decision. My boss would allow me to take an early lunch and bring Chantal home to the sitter. Everything was wonderful. Chantal was a normal four-year-old enjoying life.

The summer following Chantal's fourth birthday is when our lives changed forever. For two nights in a row, Chantal woke up complaining of back pain. It never bothered her during the day, so I called her pediatrician to have him check it out. Her appointment was scheduled for Friday morning. The doctor advised me to go straight to the hospital and have her back x-rayed and once that was done, come back to his office so he could examine her. While examining her, he told me he didn't feel anything and that we would have to wait for the results of the X-ray. He also told me not to worry. On our way home I felt a little less stressed. When John and Thomas came home, I told them what had occurred during our visit to the doctor. John tried to reassure me everything would be okay.

It was our July long weekend. We had made plans on the Saturday to spend the day in Toronto with my sister Carolle and my nephew James, who was a few years older than Chantal. We thought it would be a great time to take the children to visit Ontario Place. It was a beautiful sunny day, not a cloud in the sky. Chantal couldn't wait for her aunt and her cousin to arrive. They arrived early enough that we had time to sit and have a coffee in the backyard before we left. Chantal and James were playing and having a great old time while Carolle and I were catching up on the news. My sister lived in Buffalo, so unfortunately we did not see each other as often as we would have liked. On occasions we would spend hours on the phone, so seeing her and James that day was wonderful.

I had to go into the house to get something when the phone rang. It was the hospital. The doctor on the other end of the line told me he saw something on the X-ray and wanted us to bring Chantal in for more testing that very day. My heart jumped right to my throat. My knees felt weak. I wanted to scream out loud, "Oh God, no!" but kept quiet. The waves of fear that came over me were something I never want to experience again. I was so frightened. I could only think the worst. All I could say was, "We will be there as soon as we can."

I looked out the kitchen window and saw Carolle, Thomas, and John sitting there. I could see Chantal and James running around having fun. Watching her gave me such sadness. I knew I had to calm myself before I went outside. I went to the back door and asked John if he could come into the house for a minute. I couldn't hold it in any longer. I started to cry as I was telling him about the phone call. He also looked worried. John took me in his arms and tried to console me. "Let's wait until we get to the hospital and talk to the doctor. Right now we need to go outside and tell the kids we can't go to Toronto." We took a deep breath, composed ourselves, and went outside. Once I was in the yard, I wanted to grab Chantal and hold her tight, but I did not want to scare her. Instead we had to tell the kids we were going to the hospital, not Toronto.

We had to explain to Chantal in a way she would understand the reason she needed to go to the hospital. I told her the doctor needed to do more tests to find out why her back was hurting. She was very disappointed. I told her we would take her to Toronto another time. My telling her this seemed to help the situation. I turned my head towards Thomas and saw that he too looked worried. I felt bad we had to change the plans, but it could not be helped. Carolle tried hard to hold back her tears. With sadness in her eyes, she told us to go, that she would look after things around the house. I was glad my sister Carolle was with me that day.

Scared and anxious, we arrived at the hospital. We went right to the nurse's desk; they were expecting us. The doctor I spoke with on the phone had already told the nurse we were on our way. To our surprise, he did neglect to tell me Chantal was going to be admitted. I was not prepared for this. Had I known she was going to have to stay, I would have packed her a bag. Once all the paperwork was completed, the nurse brought Chantal to her room and made her comfortable. Another nurse came in a few minutes later, hooked her up to an IV, and then drew some of Chantal's blood. Shortly after that the doctor on call came into the room. He introduced himself and told us they were going to do just a few more tests.

They suggested it could be some kind of a viral infection. They would treat it with an antibiotic. Unfortunately, this being a long weekend, the tests would not be done until Tuesday. For the next two days, John, Thomas and I stayed with Chantal at the hospital. This was her first time away from home, and it was scary for her. To make her feel more at ease and less frightened, I explained we would stay with her until she fell asleep and would come right back first thing in the morning. The medication seemed to make her sleepy, so she did not mind us going home. John and I tried hard to stay positive. We chose to believe that the pain was caused by an infection, which wasn't a good thing, but it was far better than what we had to face on Tuesday.

My husband had gone to work that morning, as we assumed the test results would not be ready until later. I walked into my daughter's room, and she looked great. She had a big smile on her face as she extended her little arms. I went right to her and gave her the biggest hug and a kiss. "Hi, Mommy. I'm so happy to see you."

"Mommy is glad to see you too, dear. How are you feeling today?"

"I feel good."

"Was your back sore last night?"

"No."

That was music to my ears. I thought, *Maybe it is only an infection and the antibiotics are working.* A few minutes later I saw my daughter's pediatrician in the hall. He was heading in my direction, and his expression told me he didn't have good news. When he asked me to follow him into another room, my heart started pounding so hard it felt as though it was coming through my chest. I was alone, afraid, and wishing my husband were with me. My thoughts raced. I asked myself, *How could I have been so stupid, telling my husband it was okay for him to go to work?* I told Chantal the doctor wanted to talk to me and that I would be back to see her as soon as possible.

Here I was, alone. The doctor was about to explain the results of the tests. He told me to sit down, pointed at the X-ray on the wall, and began to show me a white film around the lower part of Chantal's vertebrae. He said, "It is a tumor. It could be cancerous. You need to take Chantal to another hospital in Hamilton for further testing and a biopsy."

My worst fears had come true. I started to cry, and the doctor tried to comfort me. But he was not the one I wanted to have near me. I was angry and scared, and mad that my husband was not here with me. I immediately left the room. I had to call John at work and tell him to come to the hospital as soon as possible. All I could think about was my beautiful little girl. She had no idea what her future held. I was heartbroken and wondered, *What can I say to my daughter? She is so little, how can she understand? How can a four-year-old child have cancer?*

Even when I was young, I found it easy to communicate with God. I have always put my trust in our Creator, and once again I needed to ask him to take care of my baby. I started to pray, *Oh my God, this cannot be happening. The doctors surely have made a mistake. Please help us and make this go away.* I can honestly say I never blamed God, but I still could not understand why this was happening to my sweet baby. I felt numb, in shock. I wanted to go off by myself and scream as loudly as I could. I wanted all of this to go away.

John seemed to take forever to get to the hospital, but I did not want to go into my daughter's room until he was by my side. Besides, I needed to compose myself, as I didn't want to frighten Chantal. John finally made it to the hospital, and I repeated what the doctor had told me. My husband was so shocked he didn't know what to say. He held me as I cried and cried. If there ever was a time we needed to be close to each other, this was it. Now we had to tell Chantal, even though she was too little to understand.

After the initial shock and we had calmed down a little, we went into Chantal's room. She was sitting up in her bed, a big smile on her face. When she saw her dad, she became excited. In her sweet little voice she said, "Hi, Daddy. I'm so glad to see you." John replied, "I'm so happy to see you too, Chantal," as he leaned over and gave her a big kiss. The moment we dreaded was upon us. We now had to explain to our sweet, innocent child that we needed to take her to another hospital, so the doctors there could do more tests to see why her back was hurting and make it all better. I can't explain it, but once again our little girl seemed to understand what was happening.

Throughout this suffering, we still had to be parents to our son, Thomas, who was sixteen years old at that time. He needed us too. Chantal's situation was heartbreaking for all the family, and we had to share the sad information with Thomas before leaving for the hospital in Hamilton. When he heard the news, he was very upset. He looked so sad. I felt awful having to inform him of this terrible news.

Looking back now, I believe it was hard on Thomas when his sister was born. There was a twelve-year difference in age, and now the fact that she was gravely ill may have made it more difficult for Thomas. He did not say much; he kept his feelings to himself. There were many times I felt guilty. I was so consumed by my own problems that I did not consider his feelings or talk to him about them.

We had no idea where this hospital was located, and while he was driving John became so nervous we entered the wrong way. The hospital where Chantal had been staying had told us to go to the third floor children's oncology ward, where they would be waiting for us. We arrived at the front desk. My husband, being anxious, thought he would make a joke and encouraged Chantal to tell the nurse she wanted a room for the night, like at a hotel. My daughter, who wasn't tall enough to reach the height of the counter, looked up at the nurse and said, "Hello, can I have a room for the night?" Everyone laughed. I smiled, but in my heart I knew her stay would be longer than one night.

At the children's oncology ward, the nurses hooked up Chantal to an IV, took some blood, and made her comfortable. The staff was very nice, but it seemed like an eternity before we spoke to a doctor. John and I were getting very anxious. It was difficult trying to keep Chantal busy and worrying at the same time. Finally, after waiting for over an hour, the oncologist came in and told us he was going to conduct some more tests, blood work, a scan, and another X-ray of her back to determine whether Chantal did have cancer and, if so, what treatments she would require. The doctor apologized for not being able to give us more news at that time. He did not want to speculate. He wanted to make sure all the results came back before he made a proper diagnosis. John and I understood we had to wait. We immediately phoned Thomas to give him the news and told him we were going to stay with his sister until she fell asleep. He told us to give her a kiss from her big brother and that he would see us when we got home.

For the next two weeks, Chantal stayed in the hospital for more blood work and more tests. She never complained and never whined. I stayed with Chantal during the day, went home for supper, and came back with my husband and son in the evening. We traveled forty-five minutes each day to be with her and stayed at the hospital until she was settled for the night. The ride home was always very quiet. No one seemed to want to talk.

We waited with anticipation for the results to come back. Waiting to find out if your child has cancer is the worst feeling you could ever experience. I had knots in my stomach; I couldn't eat or sleep. None of us could. I wanted all of this to go away. Unfortunately, it did not. Finally, after two weeks, the test results were in.

CHAPTER 2

Our Lives Are About to Change

The oncologist and a resident doctor came into Chantal's room. He asked us to follow him into another room. My heart was pounding so hard I wanted to throw up. I was so scared. The look of fear was also on John's face. The doctor looked at both of us and asked us to sit down. The room was very small, with a table, four chairs, and a book shelf. I noticed there were no windows; the only light came from the ceiling. A very strange feeling came over me. Why we were in there in the first place could explain the reason I felt that way. "All of Chantal's test results are in. It is confirmed Chantal has cancer. I am so sorry." I looked at John and started to cry. He put his arm around me to console me.

"This is not possible. How can Chantal have cancer? She is only four years old."

The doctor told us the hospital has seen an increase in children with cancer. That statement certainly did not make me feel any better. "I can't begin to imagine what you're feeling." He then explained, "The tumor is wrapped around the middle part of Chantal's spine. It is called a neuroblastoma. We will need to do a biopsy, analyze it to make sure. Once that is done, it will help us determine which protocol to use. We will then know how to proceed with the treatment." In other words, they needed to decide the best way to destroy the monster that inhabited Chantal's body. The nightmare was just about to begin for our sweet, innocent child.

I didn't know how to respond to the doctor. I felt numb with fear. I could not believe what I had just heard. All I could think about was my daughter and what she would have to go through. I did not want to be in that room. I wanted to be with Chantal. Your whole life changes the moment you receive such devastating news.

The surgery for the biopsy was scheduled for the next day. How on earth were we going to explain this to our daughter? She was so little; we did not want to frighten her.

Holding back my tears I sat down beside Chantal. I looked at my beautiful little girl. "Honey, tomorrow morning the doctor is going to give you something to put you to sleep. They will make a little cut on your back and remove a piece from the lump that is causing your back to hurt. They have to do this to make you all better. You will not feel the pain. You may hurt when you wake up, but the nurses will give you something to make it better." God or her angels must have helped her understand. It was as though she knew this had to be done for her to get better. It had to have been scary, and yet she made it seem as though it was just a regular routine. I have never seen a child with such courage. We told her we would be right here waiting for her after the operation. We stayed with her until she fell asleep, then left.

That night once again we had to inform Thomas of this devastating news. His sister had cancer. There was no easy way to tell him. He was waiting for us but this time had no idea we had received the diagnosis. When we got into the house, I went straight to his room and gave him the news. He was devastated; he couldn't believe it. I hugged him and told him I loved him and that somehow we would get through this.

That morning we sat with Chantal until it was time for her surgery. We told Chantal how much we loved her and what a brave little girl she was. We promised her we would bring her a treat the next day. All she asked for was an Arby's. Chantal had a wonderful appetite, and she especially loved an Arby's roast beef sandwich. The fact that Chantal knew we were bringing her the sandwich meant she wouldn't focus on the pain. John and I waited with great anticipation. The surgery was over; Chantal was in recovery. She was a little groggy and a little sore, but once she was fully awake, all she talked about was her Arby's. She couldn't wait until the next day. To keep her mind off what had just happened to her, we talked about her little friends and what she was going to do when she got out of the hospital. The nurses kept her medicated, which made her pretty sleepy. We stayed by her side until she was fast asleep for the night, then left.

The next day we arrived at the hospital around lunchtime. We headed straight to Chantal's room. We knew Chantal was waiting patiently for her treat. She was so happy. She ate the whole thing, never once complaining of discomfort or what they had done to her. The whole day John, Thomas, and I kept her busy playing games and reading her stories.

The next stage of Chantal's care involved the doctors figuring out what protocol to give her, and for how long. The biopsy would help the doctors determine this. Once again the oncologist brought us into a room. This room was a little more pleasant. It had a window. The rays of the sunlight reflected on the window pane. You could feel the warmth of the sun in the room. The doctor began to inform us on how he was going to treat Chantal's cancer. "After consulting with my colleagues, we agreed on which protocol would be best to treat Chantal's cancer. Although at this time there is only a 45 percent cure rate for this type of cancer."

"A 45 percent cure rate? That doesn't sound very hopeful."

"We feel very optimistic that this treatment will work best for your daughter."

"How will you treat this cancer?"

"We will begin with thirty days of radiation to shrink the tumor, and a year and a half of chemotherapy, administered every twenty-one days. During her chemotherapy sessions Chantal will have to be admitted the night prior to the treatment. The radiation treatments will be done Monday through Friday at a different hospital. We will have to surgically insert a Hickman tube in Chantal's neck to administer the chemotherapy drug."

"What is a Hickman tube?"

"We will cut a small opening on the side of Chantal's neck and another one below her breast. A small tube is inserted into the opening on the neck and will come out of the opening below the breast. The chemotherapy drug will be administered through this tube, preventing any burning. Also, if the nurses need to administer anything else throughout all the treatments, it will be much easier on Chantal."

The thought of that poison going into my baby was very disturbing to me. Our family had no idea what we were about to face.

Chantal being only four years old, so little, and weighing just thirty-five pounds, a special mold had to be made to lay her body on, so that when she went in for radiation the mold would prevent her from moving during treatment. It was very important that the patient lie still, in order for the rays to hit the right spot. While we were in the doctor's office and she was explaining what needed to be done, the doctor happened to notice Chantal sitting very still. She turned to me. "Is Chantal always this well behaved? She is so quiet."

"Yes, she is a very good little girl."

"Let me try something." The doctor asked Chantal to lie down on the table and not to move until she said it was okay. My baby did not move an inch or even twitch. The doctor was amazed. She told my husband and me, "In all the years I have been doing this work, I have never come across a child her age sit still like this." She told us that even some grownups can't sit still for that length of time. The doctor decided that she did not need to make this mold and to come back on Monday for her first radiation treatment. Once again Chantal's angels stepped in to help make it easier for all of us.

Now that we knew what to expect, we had to tell our family and work. When this nightmare began, John and I had decided not to tell anyone in our family about Chantal's illness. Why worry them until we had all the facts? It was now time to make the calls. We both dreaded this moment, but we knew it had to be done. Being an only child, John's main concern was telling his parents. I had to call my older brother Michel and his wife Nicole, my mom and dad, all of whom reside in Quebec City. I had to tell my sisters, Ginette from St. Catharines and Carolle from Buffalo. Everyone's reaction was the same. They were all devastated and so sad to hear that Chantal was so sick. They said they would send prayers for our family and be there for us no matter what.

I then called my employer, who was very understanding. She told me not to worry, to keep her posted, and to come back when the time was right. This was a huge relief for me, to know that I could keep my focus on Chantal. John's employer was also very understanding. At the same time, I was also concerned about Thomas. Because he was sixteen years old, I knew he understood what was happening to his sister. Unfortunately, it was very difficult for John, Thomas, and me to share our feelings or to even discuss Chantal.

When a loved one is diagnosed with an illness, the family may find it difficult to share their feelings or to even want to talk about the situation. Looking back I only wish I had insisted we talk about it more openly.

It was a Monday morning in July. We did not get much sleep that weekend. We had to be at Henderson Hospital, forty-five minutes away, for Chantal's first dose of radiation. Her appointment was scheduled for ten o'clock. I was very nervous. I couldn't eat. John and Chantal had a light breakfast. We all agreed it was not necessary for Thomas to come with us that day. Since we had been there on Friday, we knew exactly where to go. The attending nurse looked up and said, "Hello. Can I help you?"

"Hi. My daughter, Chantal Commerford, has an appointment for ten o'clock."

"Yes, please have a seat in the waiting room. A nurse will be here shortly to come and get Chantal."

The minutes seemed like hours. It was an old hospital, with old furniture. The room felt cold and eerie. I did not want to be there. Finally, the nurse arrived. I thought, *Our baby's nightmare is about to begin.* My heart sank to the pit of my stomach. I felt so helpless. With tears in my eyes I gave Chantal a big hug and a kiss. I did not want to let her go. By the look on John's face, I knew he felt the same way. He in turn gave Chantal the same. With a lump in my throat, I said, "Mommy and Daddy will be right here waiting for you. We love you." Because of the gravity of the treatment no one was allowed in that area. I felt guilty not being there with Chantal to hold her hand. John and I sat in silence as we waited for our daughter to return.

What was only going to take a few minutes seemed like an eternity. I had my eyes focused on the clock when I heard

Chantal's sweet little voice say, "Hi, Mommy and Daddy. I'm back." We were both so happy to see her. The nurse told us she did fine, never once moved. I was so proud of my little girl. I picked her up and held her close to me. We thanked the nurse and told her we would see her tomorrow. We couldn't wait to return home.

The doctor had previously explained the procedure for Chantal's radiation treatment. She seemed so happy I felt it best not to question her. When we got home Chantal ate some lunch and went to play with her friends. John and I were relieved that the first day was behind us. We were back again on Tuesday for another session. Wednesday's treatment was put on hold. Chantal had to be admitted to the hospital to have her Hickman put in.

On Monday night we sat down and began to explain to Chantal what was going to take place on Wednesday morning. We did not want to frighten her. "Chantal, do you remember the last time the doctors put you to sleep and made a little cut on your back?"

"Yes, Mommy."

"This time the doctor has to make a small opening on your neck and another one below your booby." I took my hand and showed her the exact spots on her body so she would understand.

"Why are they going to do this to me, Mommy?"

Sadly, I said, "Honey to get rid of the pain in your back the doctors have to put some medicine through this tube to make you all better."

"Will it hurt?"

"A little. Just like the last time, the nurse will give you medication to take away your pain if it hurts."

"I want you and Daddy to be there after I wake up."

"Don't worry, dear. Mommy and Daddy will be right beside you."

We had arrived at McMaster Hospital at eight o'clock. Her surgery was scheduled for nine o'clock. Once Chantal was all settled on her bed, I asked her, "Chantal, do you remember what Mommy said to you on Monday, and what the doctor was going to do to you today?"

She said, "Yes, Mommy, I remember." She was such a brave little girl, she didn't even cry. I was so grateful. At that moment John and I were so proud of our little girl. We stayed by her side until they came and took her to surgery. John, Thomas, and I waited with great anticipation.

The procedure took less than an hour, and because it was day surgery Chantal would be able to go home that same day. The doctor came and told us all went very well. Chantal was in recovery, feeling a little sore and groggy. We could go in and stay with her until her discharge. When we entered the room, she smiled. She then started to cry. It was easy to understand why, considering what she had just gone through. We sat with her; very few words were spoken. Later that day Chantal was discharged from the hospital.

Thursday morning we were back to Henderson Hospital for another treatment of radiation. I wish the doctors would have given Chantal a few days off after the surgery. It couldn't be helped; it was crucial this tumor be destroyed as soon as possible. We travelled back and forth for Chantal's radiation treatment every day for three weeks. During that time my daughter was fine. She had a good appetite, no pain or illness. She played with friends in the neighborhood. September was around the corner; she was looking forward to being with her little classmates at school. We were starting to feel a little less stressed. On her fourth week of radiation, the doctor started her on chemotherapy, and that was when our family life became a hell.

Because of the type of cancer Chantal had, our little girl needed to be admitted to the hospital the night before. The nurses would hook her up to an IV drip, and this way she would be ready for her treatment the next morning. The session lasted the whole day, and if all went well, we could go home the following morning. Our daughter's first chemotherapy treatment was scheduled for August 7, a Monday morning, which meant I had to take her in on Sunday. Because it was summer, the days were still fairly long. I waited until after supper to leave for the hospital. I packed a change of clothes for Chantal and me for the following day. It was now time to leave. My husband and son both gave Chantal a hug and a kiss. Leaving John and Thomas behind was upsetting to me. Seeing the sadness in their eyes as Chantal and I drove off was even worse. I realized at that moment I needed to put all my focus on Chantal.

The hospital room was pleasant. It provided us with a sink, a television, and a couch that converted into a bed. This enabled me to stay with my daughter through the night. Thank God for that. I don't know that I could have left her side. When Chantal was first admitted to McMaster Hospital for her biopsy, we met a lot of the nurses on staff. They were all so nice to us that I knew Chantal would be well cared for. Once my daughter was admitted, the nurse took us directly to Chantal's room. She then proceeded to take her vitals and hook her up to an IV. Chantal was very calm at this point. Once all of this was done, I lay down beside my baby, and we watched television until she fell asleep.

We woke up to a beautiful sunny day. However, because of what Chantal and I were about to face, I could not appreciate its beauty. I did not sleep a wink that night. Chantal was awake and in good spirits. I asked her how she slept. She replied, "I slept good Mommy." I was certainly glad to hear that, especially knowing what she was about to face. All of sudden reality set in. *Oh my God, the nurse is going to come in any minute now and hook Chantal up to that poison.* I had to change my negative thoughts. I told myself, *Louise, these drugs are going to destroy Chantal's tumor and make her well.* That was the only thought I needed to focus on.

The oncologist and the resident doctors were making their usual rounds. When they arrived at Chantal's room, the oncologist asked, "How are you doing?"

I replied, "Chantal had a good night's sleep. I am a bit anxious and can't wait for the day to be over."

He said, "I understand." He also asked me if it was all right for the resident doctors to ask me a few questions. I told him it was fine.

The resident doctor proceeded to ask me, "When did Chantal first start having this pain?" I told him in early July Chantal was complaining of back pain. The pain bothered her for only two nights. It never bothered her during the day. I went to her pediatrician, and he requested an X-ray be taken. The result on the film showed a lesion on her spine. I told him everything that led us to being here today. *Why is he asking me to repeat what they already know?* I could not understand why I needed to repeat this information. All of this was in their files. He wrote a few notes down in his pad and thanked me. The oncologist then told me the nurse would be in shortly to administer Chantal's first dose of chemotherapy drugs.

I couldn't wait for this day to be over. I was feeling sick to my stomach. I had to stay strong for Chantal. She was the one having to go through this. A few minutes later the nurse walked in holding the bag containing the medicine. I noticed it was orange. Chantal never uttered a word; she just lay there quiet. It wasn't long before she fell asleep. The treatment would last most of the day.

Even though Chantal slept through all of it, I dared not leave her side. The nurse was nice enough to bring me a sandwich. I stared at Chantal as she lay there so peaceful and so still. I watched the bag as it slowly emptied. Chantal woke up a few times sick to her stomach. It pained me to see her having to go through this. I wiped her face and told her how much I loved her. It wasn't too long after that she went back to sleep. The nurse came in periodically to check on her vitals and make sure all was well. It was now four o'clock in the afternoon. I glanced at the bag that held her life-saving drug. It was empty.

Finally, the first treatment was officially over. Soon after that the nurse came in and disconnected the bag. Chantal was still asleep. About an hour later she woke up saying she was hungry. The nurse brought in her tray. Chantal couldn't eat much; it was difficult for her to keep her food down. Her little stomach was upset. We watched television for a few hours and then fell asleep.

The next morning Chantal was able to eat her breakfast. We couldn't wait for the doctor to make his rounds. I was told if Chantal's blood count came back normal, we could go home. If her blood count was low, that would mean her immune system would not be able to fight any infection and she would need to have a transfusion. That meant we would have to stay an extra day. The doctor finally came in the room, and he examined Chantal, who seemed fine. He told us the report came back from the lab, her counts were good, and we could go home. We were both thrilled. We said our good-byes and left.

For the days to follow, we watched Chantal feel the effects of the drugs. She started to lose her appetite. She was sick to her stomach, her throat became irritated from heaving, she suffered abdominal pain, and she became so weak the doctor had to put her last week of radiation on hold. After a few weeks of Chantal suffering from severe pain, the doctor was finally able to administer medication to ease some of her agony. Chantal was now able to finish her last five sessions of radiation. On Friday, that part of the treatment was finally over for our sweet little girl. We never liked going to that hospital. In fact we dreaded it. The atmosphere was not very pleasant, which is understandable, considering why we were there.

It was now time for Chantal's second chemotherapy treatment. Just like the first time, we went to the hospital the night before. The next day she slept through the treatment. That evening she was sick a few times but rested comfortably throughout the night. The next morning Chantal's blood count showed normal, we were able to go home. The following week was again hell for my daughter. She could hardly eat. She was feverish. She was vomiting and still experiencing abdominal pains. She looked so frail. All she could do was lie there. It took every bit of energy she had left to get up and walk around. It was deeply upsetting to see her suffer. As a parent, it is difficult to watch your child in pain. You want to take it all away and make it better. It was an extremely difficult time, and it was just beginning. I prayed to God to ease her pain and make her better.

Seeing my baby suffering so much agony was heart wrenching. This was a time in my life when I wished I could have performed hands-on healing on my daughter and rid her of her pain. I only wish I could have done then what I can do now.

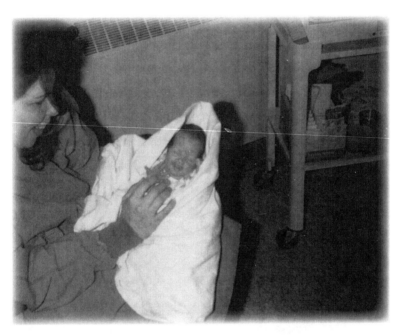

Chantal 3 weeks old weighing 4lbs 2oz.

Chantal at the age of 3 years old

Chantal age 5 six months into her treatments

Chantal age 5 wearing her curly wig

Luckily, Chantal had a clinic visit that week. She was still experiencing abdominal pain, and I wanted it looked after. It was necessary to visit the clinic once a month for Chantal's routine follow-up. The clinic was on the third floor of the hospital. Before going to the clinic, we always had to arrive an hour earlier, go to the first floor, and have Chantal's blood work done. This way the results would be upstairs in the clinic by the time Chantal was examined.

At each visit the nurse weighed Chantal and took her height measurement. The oncologist would then examine Chantal. He would feel her abdomen and other areas of the body for any unusual signs. If I had any concerns, this was the perfect time to address them. The nurse directed us to the examining room and told us the doctor would be there shortly. McMaster was a lot newer than Henderson Hospital. The room was very cheerful and bright. Being a children's clinic, the walls had cute pictures, which made it more tolerable for the little ones to look at while waiting for their check-up. There was a desk with two chairs and, of course, the examining table. The atmosphere was pleasant.

We didn't have to wait too long before the doctor entered the room. "Hello, how are we doing today?"

I replied, "Chantal has been having some severe abdominal pain. The pain started right after her first chemotherapy treatment. The pain has since become more severe. I hate to see her suffering. I am really concerned; you have to do something." While the doctor was pushing on Chantal's abdomen, she cried with pain. I put my hand on my forehead to cover the tears in my eyes.

He turned to me. "I feel she has a lot of stools in her intestines. Her problem could be she is constipated. This will cause the muscles to contract. Does she have a regular bowel movement?"

"She doesn't go every day."

"I really believe this problem is causing Chantal's pain."

He looked at Chantal and said, "Don't worry dear. We will make you feel better." He then turned to me. "I will set up an appointment for Chantal to see a gastroenterologist, a doctor who specializes in the intestines. In the meantime I will prescribe a stool softener, which will help her."

"It never occurred to me that her stools could be causing such pain."

"Yes, one of the drugs can cause this problem. Chantal should have been put on stool softeners before her first treatment."

"I recall them asking me if she was regular. I told them yes; at that time she was."

"It's unfortunate that this happened to Chantal, but we will make her feel better."

I thought to myself, *Yes, but it's my daughter who is suffering.* I was still grateful he was going to look after the problem. He told me to go back to the sitting area while he arranged to schedule the appointment. I felt a sigh of relief. I thanked him, and we left the room.

The clinic doctor was able to have the appointment with the specialist scheduled for eleven o'clock the next morning. Whether the doctor explained the severity of Chantal's pain to the nurse at the specialist's office or whether someone in heaven was watching out for her, I don't know. All I could say was, "Thank you, thank you." With the help of the laxative, Chantal's pain seemed to subside that night.

The next day we arrived in plenty of time in the hopes that they might see Chantal earlier than scheduled. The secretary told us to have a seat in the waiting room. The nurse arrived and brought us to the examining room. Within minutes the doctor walked in. He introduced himself and asked me to explain everything that led to Chantal having this pain. He proceeded to examine Chantal. He then turned to me saying, "Has Chantal had regular bowel movements throughout her treatments? I am feeling a lot of stools in Chantal's abdomen. To rule out other possibilities, I would like Chantal to have an X-ray taken of her abdomen. I will give you a requisition form, go the main floor to the X-ray department, and have it done. Then come back and see me."

The waiting room in the X-ray department was pretty quiet, so we were able to have it done right away. We went right back to the specialist's office and waited for our turn. This time we waited for an hour, but I did not care. The doctor could have told us to come back another day for the X-ray. I was happy he was looking after Chantal that day. I was feeling nervous. Chantal was just sitting there quietly. She was so strong and brave. The nurse arrived and brought us back into the examining room. "Just as I thought, Chantal's problem is constipation. You will both go back to the clinic; I will call the nurse have her give Chantal a suppository and an enema to rid Chantal of the old stools. You will then be free to go home. Chantal will have to remain on stool softeners until the end of her chemotherapy." Everything went according to plan. It was then three o'clock in the afternoon, and we were heading home.

John and Thomas were both anxious to find out what took place that day. After I explained everything to them, they were both so relieved. With the aid of the stool softeners, Chantal rarely experienced abdominal pain, and when she did it was never again as severe.

After Chantal's third chemotherapy treatment, we were allowed to go home. Once again, her blood count was normal. Unfortunately, the days to follow were not so good. Chantal was heaving a lot after her treatment. Her throat became very sore. She could hardly swallow. She did not have much of an appetite, and she was losing weight. Chantal was actually afraid to eat; she told us it burned. I immediately called the clinic to make an appointment. I could not wait for her scheduled follow-up. We were able to come in the next day.

In the meantime, all Chantal could eat was pudding and Jell-O. Once the clinic doctor examined Chantal's throat, he concluded she would need an endoscopy. Chantal would have a scope inserted down her throat and into the stomach area. This would help the doctor determine what was causing the burning feeling in her throat. We were not so lucky this time; we had to wait almost a week for this test. It pained us to see our daughter having to suffer once again. She was so little that she could not afford to lose any more weight. Chantal was still afraid to eat, afraid of the burning she would endure when she swallowed.

She tried so hard to eat. It broke my heart to see her like this. It was also very upsetting for her dad and her brother.

I continued to feed her soft foods, but the burning continued. I kept praying for all of this to end soon. Besides the suffering Chantal was experiencing, we now had to explain to her what the doctor needed to do to make her throat better. The only thing we could tell her was they were going to insert a tube with a camera down her throat. There really was no easy way to explain this to a four-year-old. She started to cry. "No, Mommy. It's going to hurt." I told her the doctor was going to give her some medicine to relax her so that she would not feel the tube going down. She still seemed to be afraid. I picked her up and held her close to me. "Chantal, I am so sorry you have to go through this. You have to do this, so the doctor can make your throat all better, so you will be able to eat again." It took a little while, but she finally calmed down.

The day finally arrived. My husband and I couldn't wait to get to the hospital. We parked the car and immediately went to the area where they do the endoscopy. The nurse took Chantal in right away. She also told me I could come along and stay in the room with Chantal until the doctor came in to do the test. I was so happy I was allowed to be by Chantal's side during this difficult time. The nurse administered a mild sedative to relax Chantal. It did not take long for the effect to take place. Chantal became very relaxed, almost falling asleep. The doctor entered the room, introduced himself, and told me he would talk to me as soon as he was finished.

One thing I had to learn throughout this whole ordeal was patience. We always had to wait during the appointments and during the tests. You had no choice. All you could do was appreciate the times you did not have to wait so long. Mind you, they were few and far between.

John and I waited patiently for the doctor to appear. Approximately an hour had gone by. We saw the nurse come towards us. She told us to follow her back into the endoscopy room. The test was all done. Chantal was waiting for us. She was very happy to see us. John and I ran to her and gave her a big hug. The doctor explained, "Chantal's throat is burning because it is raw from all the heaving she has been doing after her treatment. I will give her medicine to help heal her throat. She should start to feel better within a few days of taking the medicine."

"Thank you so much, doctor. That's great to hear." We were both so very proud of our daughter. Within a few days the medicine was already working, and Chantal's burning was almost all gone.

The other issue we needed to watch for was keeping the Hickman tube clear. The part of the tube that came out of her chest required flushing every week; if it crystallized, it meant Chantal had an infection. This would mean Chantal would need to be admitted to the hospital for ten to fourteen days to clear this infection. I was always nervous before I removed the bandage. I would say a prayer asking God that there be no redness around the opening. If there was, it meant she had an infection and we would head for the hospital. Throughout the year and a half of treatments, Chantal had to be admitted only four times for infections. By contrast, due to her low blood count after chemotherapy, she had to remain in the hospital eleven times (for blood transfusions).

While Chantal was in the hospital, there was one nurse in particular who took a shine to Chantal. She fell in love with my daughter instantly, and my daughter felt the same about her. Her name was Shelley. She was a petite woman, very pretty, standing about five feet tall, with short blonde hair and large framed glasses. Shelley was always smiling. She was not only beautiful on the outside; inside she was a loving, caring, compassionate person who gave herself to these children. What an angel she was! Whenever Chantal had to be admitted to the hospital, she would always say, "I hope Shelley is working today." When she was on duty, Chantal would be so excited. Not that she didn't like the other nurses; they were all so wonderful to Chantal. She simply loved Shelley more. While on duty Shelley always took very good care of my baby. Even after a treatment when Chantal was feeling sick, having Shelley there made it more bearable.

There was a time I will never forget. Chantal had to go into the hospital for chemotherapy. To give me a break, Shelley was kind enough to come in on her day off and spend it with Chantal. I don't know too many nurses who would do this. I was so grateful to Shelley. Even after Chantal's treatments, for the years to follow Chantal spent weekends in Shelley's home. They played board games together. She read books to Chantal. Shelley even took my daughter to African Lions Safari with a friend from work and her two daughters Chantal's age. She always had a wonderful time with Shelley. Years later Shelley met Ron. The two of them decided to get married. Chantal was invited to Shelley's wedding. It was September 1994. Chantal was twelve years old at that time. This meant so much to my daughter. Unfortunately for Chantal, Shelley and Ron moved to Colorado, so they never saw each other again. The hours they spent together were deeply treasured by my daughter.

Chantal and Shelley kept in contact for years and then they lost touch. This will happen. You have someone special who comes into your life for a certain time, a certain purpose, and once that event in your life is over, that person no longer needs to be there. So you move on. That part of your journey is over, and you move on to the next phase in your life. There is always a reason that people come in and out of our lives. There is a lesson to be learned from each person, and for Shelley and Chantal, that part of their experience was over, but never forgotten.

Chantal was the one suffering the effects of the treatments, and yet it was my beautiful daughter who gave me the strength and the courage to go on. By now Chantal was thin and her skin a little pale. She was starting to lose her beautiful, brown curly locks. Chantal rarely complained or whined. She remained a fighter. Seeing Chantal deal with her illness with such courage gave me the courage to believe there was a light at the end of this dark tunnel. I was so proud of my little girl. It was now the end of August, and Chantal was feeling pretty good.

Even though we were living a nightmare, we tried to make Chantal's life as normal as possible. In September we enrolled Chantal in kindergarten. She loved going to school and playing with the children. By this time Chantal had lost all her hair, but that did not bother her at all. We had bought her a wig with curly brown hair. She was so cute; she looked like Little Orphan Annie. But Chantal preferred to go to school bald. Kids can be very cruel. Chantal came home telling me some of the children laughed at her. It broke my heart that they could do that to her. I explained to my daughter that the kids that were mean did not understand she was sick. I then asked her if other little boys and girls played with her. She told me they did. I told her from now on just play with them and to never mind the other children. The days to follow were bearable for Chantal. Eventually it stopped.

Growing up, we have all experienced someone in our lives who do not like us. That is their choice. We can't allow how other people perceive us bother us. We must let it go and be grateful for the friends who do care for us. That is how my young daughter saw this lesson. She did not react to those kids, because there were many who liked her for who she was.

It was almost the end of September. The leaves on the trees were beautiful shades of red-orange and yellow. Chantal was going in to the hospital for another treatment. She had the usual side effects. Her blood count was very low, which meant she needed a transfusion, so we couldn't go home until the next day. After a few days at home, the effects of the treatment became worse. Chantal had a temperature of 101. She had no appetite, she was vomiting, and she had severe diarrhea. I called the clinic to make an appointment. They told me to bring her in right away. I quickly packed a bag, and we immediately left for the hospital.

The clinic doctor examined Chantal. When he saw the results of her blood count came back really low, he decided to have her admitted. The blood work also showed an infection. Chantal had to be put on antibiotics. This also meant Chantal would not be able to leave her room, lest she spread the infection to the other children. By the evening the diarrhea finally stopped. The vomiting continued throughout the night. My poor baby tried so hard to keep down the little bit of food she was able to eat. It was very upsetting to see her so sick. Things just seemed to be getting worse. We hardly slept that night. Chantal was exhausted.

It was around seven o'clock in the morning, time for the shift change. One of the new nurses on duty came in with Chantal's tray. She was able to eat some of it and keep it down. I was very pleased. Soon after that another nurse came in to draw more blood. Thank God for the Hickman, otherwise Chantal's arm would have been full of needle marks and bruised.

Around ten o'clock the oncologist and the residents were doing their rounds. Another resident started asking me the same questions I had been asked several times before. I lost it. I was so upset because of what Chantal went through the night before. I rudely told him to look in their files, that I wasn't about to repeat Chantal's history anymore. That was not like me to be so rude. I couldn't help it. I had had enough of the questions. I just couldn't take it anymore. The resident apologized for upsetting me and went and stood behind the other doctors.

The oncologist proceeded to say, "Chantal's blood count is much higher today, but her hemoglobin is low; she will need another transfusion. We will see how Chantal is doing after that." I felt bad because of what I said to the resident. I apologized to the doctors as they were leaving the room. He understood; he knew what I was going through.

The next day the side effects seemed to be under control. Chantal was eating and able to keep it down. It was around one o'clock in the afternoon, and Chantal was taking a nap. I needed to have a break. Just outside the ward was a family room with a television and coffee maker. Most of the mothers and fathers would go there to relax, release some of the stress, and simply talk. *As much as you want to be with your child during this difficult period, you also need time for yourself.* This was the perfect place for that.

The rest of the week was much calmer. Chantal was getting better and stronger. We kept busy watching television, doing puzzles, and reading books. We were both sleeping better at night. After our spending nine days in the hospital, Chantal's blood work finally came back normal, and she was discharged. We couldn't get home fast enough. She looked forward to seeing her daddy and brother and going back to school to see her little friends.

After this last treatment it seemed the worst was behind us. Halloween was just around the corner. Chantal was so looking forward to wearing her costume. She had decided on an angel costume with wings and a halo. It was cool that night, and I talked her into wearing her little wig. She looked like a little angel. We only went up the street, as I did not want Chantal to get tired. I was so grateful that she was well enough to enjoy that night.

Because of Chantal's immune system, John and I agreed to keep Chantal out of school. We couldn't risk her getting sick. She was not happy about that. She knew that meant she couldn't play with her little classmates. We explained to her that even though she was not able to go to school, when her blood count was high enough she could play with the two little friends from across the street. She seemed okay with that.

It is bad enough your child has to suffer through this illness. It's also very difficult for a parent to have to take something or someone away that makes them happy and helps them to forget their problems.

During the November treatment Chantal experienced the usual side effects. Her blood count remained fairly normal. Two weeks after her treatment, an ultrasound and an MRI were taken to see how much the tumor had shrunk. It was a Wednesday morning. Chantal had a follow-up at the clinic the following Monday. John, Thomas, and I tried to stay positive the tests would come back showing the tumor was smaller. Nevertheless, it was nerve-racking. We couldn't wait for Monday morning.

CHAPTER 3

Wonderful News

Once we arrived at the hospital, John, Chantal, and I sat down and waited anxiously for our name to be called. Within a few minutes the nurse came to get us. We followed her to the examining room. She took Chantal's height and weight. I held on to Chantal until the doctor arrived. The oncologist walked in and said, "I have wonderful news. Chantal's tumor has shrunk almost half the size." John and I both looked at each other with a big smile on our faces. We were so relieved. "Thank you, God, for taking care of my baby." I explained to Chantal what the doctor had just told us so she could understand. She was just as happy as John and I. The doctor proceeded to examine Chantal. He asked us if we had any questions. "No, we are just so happy and so grateful, thank you so much," we told him.

When we got home we told Thomas the wonderful news. He was also very excited for his little sister. We then called the family, and they too were thrilled.

Chantal turned five years old at the end of November. It was a time to celebrate. We invited the whole family to share in the celebration of her birthday and the good news from the doctor. Chantal was so excited to see her cousins and of course to open the wonderful gifts she received. Knowing the treatments were working, seeing our little girl laughing and enjoying herself, was the best gift our family could ever receive. December was also a great month for Chantal and the family. She was feeling really good and looking forward to Christmas. Helping to decorate the tree meant so much to Chantal. I wanted this to be a special Christmas for all of us.

Coming from a French Canadian family, Christmas Eve was the biggest night for celebration at my parents. I remember the 1979 Christmas gathering at Mom and Dad's, the last before they moved back to Quebec. There were John and I and Thomas, who was then eight years old. My older brother Michel, his wife Nicole, their son Marc, also eight years old, and their daughter Annie, four years old. My older sister Carolle, and her husband David. My sister Ginette, her husband John, and daughter Jennifer, six years old. The adults attended midnight mass while my mom watched the little ones.

After church we would go back to my parents and sit down to a huge feast my dad had spent the whole day preparing. It consisted of turkey and all the trimmings, ham, and of course our traditional homemade meat pie. We exchanged gifts and listened to Christmas carols. Listening to "Ave Maria" and "O Holy Night" by the famous tenor Enrico Caruso was a very special moment for my father. We all had to sit there very quiet. Those years are great memories for me. After my parents moved to Quebec, Carolle, Ginette, and I decided that on the twenty-fourth of December we were going to continue the family tradition and take turns having Christmas Eve. This Christmas was my turn. I made sure it was going to be the most memorable for Chantal and the rest of our family.

It was January, the start of a new year. We were very fortunate that winter that the roads remained safe for driving. For the many months that followed, Chantal continued her treatments and having the usual side effects. On occasion Thomas would relieve me and spend the night with his sister. She loved having her big brother around. She would go around the ward telling the nurses and the children, "This is my big brother, Thomas. He is going to stay with me tonight." Other than the few times Chantal was admitted for infections and blood transfusions, she did not experience any major setbacks until her treatment in early May.

It was a Thursday Chantal was admitted to the hospital for her twelfth chemotherapy. Once again after treatment Chantal had to have another transfusion. This was her eighth one. She was then discharged, and we were able to go home. The following Monday, Chantal had a follow-up appointment at the clinic. Her blood work came back showing her counts were again low. She was given platelets. These are found in the blood and are involved in clotting of the blood. By Friday Chantal was not feeling well. She had absolutely no energy, and a temperature of 101. I was getting concerned. Even with Tylenol, Chantal's fever would not go down. Throughout the night I kept getting up and taking Chantal's temperature; it had gone down one degree. By morning her temperature had gone back up. I called the hospital and explained to the doctor on call what had taken place earlier that week. He told me to bring her in as soon as possible.

After examining Chantal the doctor thought it was best to admit her. Once again Chantal was put in isolation until they were able to find the cause of the fever. I was prepared to stay with my daughter as long as it took for her to recover from this setback. The nurses coming in the room to check her vitals and giving her Tylenol for her fever made for a restless night. As much as we did not want to be there, I knew this was the safest place for my baby.

The night duty nurse came in to check on Chantal one more time before the end of her shift. I was awake at that time. She noticed Chantal had spots on her face and torso. She immediately left the room to get the resident on call. I got up, looked at Chantal, and became frightened when I noticed her spots. She looked as though she had the measles. Soon the doctor arrived to examine Chantal. He asked me what symptoms Chantal had experienced since her last treatment. I explained to the resident everything that had occurred since her chemotherapy. "We will need to do some more blood work. Chantal's body may be reacting to an infection. As soon as we get the results, we will know more." You would think by now I would have been used to the waiting. Worrying about the unknown is what made the waiting seem so long.

Due to the fever and the spots that covered her body, Chantal had to be transferred to a different ward and kept in isolation. On this ward each patient was assigned the same nurse throughout the shift. The blood work finally came back. The doctors remained puzzled. The oncologist told me he would have to do more testing. He could not understand why her body was reacting this way. This was not her first transfusion. Every inch of her body, even the inside of her mouth, was covered in lesions. Her fever remained high. She had no appetite. On top of all of this, I had to tell my little girl I couldn't stay overnight with her because of the isolation. Chantal started to cry. She did not want me to leave she became very upset. This broke my heart: was this nightmare ever going to end?

To comfort Chantal I held her close to me. I told her I would be back first thing in the morning. I also promised Chantal I would stay with her until she fell asleep. She seemed to understand why I couldn't stay with her. Around eight o'clock that evening the nurse came into the room to administer Chantal's medication and within minutes she fell asleep. I waited a short while to make sure she was asleep, and then I left. When I got into my car, I started to cry and prayed to God to look after my baby. I continued to cry all the way home. John and Thomas were both anxiously waiting for my arrival. I gave them all the news I had. John told me he would come with me the following day and spend it with Chantal.

The next day we arrived at the hospital bright and early. John and I put on our gowns, masks, and gloves before we entered Chantal's room. When we walked in, we hardly recognized her.

That morning Chantal had been given prednisone. This drug is similar to cortisone. The medication caused her body to swell like a balloon. This was not our little Chantal. How could this be happening? John and I were shocked to see her this way. The nurse told us it was necessary to give her this drug to fight an allergic reaction Chantal may have had from the transfusion. We waited to see the oncologist. At this stage the doctor was still not quite sure what the cause of Chantal's spots and fever was. He assured both John and me that he was going to find a solution to this reaction and in the meantime make Chantal as comfortable as possible.

I wanted all of this to go away. The prednisone was making Chantal irritable and miserable. Once in a while she would snap at her dad and me. We simply allowed her to take her frustrations out on us. That was the least we could do. We stayed with our daughter until she fell asleep. Now we had to go home and tell Thomas the doctors were still not sure what was happening to his baby sister.

That weekend my parents happened to be coming down from Quebec to see Chantal. Carolle and her new husband Tom, from Buffalo, also came down to visit. We all geared up. My mother decided she wanted to go in first. As soon as Chantal noticed her grandmother, whom she had seen many times before, she screamed for my mom to get out of her room. My poor mother was so upset. We explained to my mom it wasn't anything she did. It was the side effects of the drug.

The family was only allowed to stay for a short visit. Everyone had their turn with Chantal while I sat with my mom.

I told my mother I would go in and speak to Chantal. Soon after, my mom and I went in together. Chantal had no idea why she reacted this way. We blame it on the fact that the drug made Chantal miserable. Her temperature was still over one hundred, she had no appetite. She had all these spots inside her mouth and all over her body. She was not feeling well and she was frightened. My poor little girl had already gone through so much. She told her grandma she was sorry. My mother understood and all was forgotten.

The doctor on duty told John and me they were going to put Chantal on piperacillin, another form of antibiotics. I felt my daughter was a human guinea peg. Almost two weeks had gone by during this whole ordeal. John and I felt helpless. Nothing the doctors administered seemed to be working. All we could do was pray the doctors would find the cause. It was a very emotional time for all our family. John and I stayed with Chantal until she fell asleep. Having the family support during this difficult time in our lives was a gift. John, Thomas, and I were so grateful.

It was Monday morning. We woke up to a beautiful sunny day. My parents had to go back home. They told us to call them as soon as there were any new developments. John and Thomas had to go back to work. I had called the hospital through the night to see how Chantal was doing. The nurse assured me Chantal was sleeping and kept comfortable. I was relieved to hear this.

Unfortunately, when I arrived at the hospital, things were not so good. Chantal's fever was high. She still had no appetite and was still covered in spots. Now her gums were bleeding, and she had diarrhea. When I saw her I felt sick to my stomach. I tried so hard to be strong for her but seeing Chantal this way brought tears to my eyes. *How much more can she endure?* I wondered. I couldn't wait to talk to the oncologist. I anxiously awaited his arrival. As soon as he approached the room, before any one of the doctors could ask me a question, I stood up and asked, "How much longer is Chantal going to suffer? You need to find out what is causing all of this."

"I am so sorry Chantal is so sick. We are doing the best we can. Our next step is to take a sample from one of the spots and have it analyzed to see if it is a viral infection. If it is, we will know how to treat it." I couldn't understand why they waited so long to take that sample. Chantal had been suffering for two weeks already. Once again we would have to wait.

A few days passed. Chantal's fever was still up and down, and they had to give her another transfusion and more platelets. This made her feel a little better; however, her gums were still sore and bleeding. Seeing Chantal this way was very disturbing. I felt helpless. By late morning the oncologist walked in the room to tell me the results were back from the lab.

"Mrs. Commerford, the results show it is not a viral infection. I know exactly what Chantal has and how we are going to treat it. We discovered Chantal has what we call GVH, graft-versus-host. Chantal received a bad batch of blood during a transfusion. Because her immune system was so low, instead of fighting the infection, the germ grew inside her. We are now able to provide her with the proper medication to get rid of the infection which invaded her body. All the suffering that Chantal has gone through made us aware of the need to radiate and remove all impurities from the blood received by donors. It was unfortunate that your daughter had to go through this ordeal, but the discovery will prevent it from happening to someone else. The nurse will be in shortly to administer the medication. Chantal should be starting to feel better soon."

"I am just so grateful you finally found out what was causing Chantal to be so sick." I thanked her; in fact, if I recall, I hugged her. I was so relieved.

I went right to my daughter to give her the good news. Looking at her frail little body, I leaned over and kissed her. I explained to her the doctors knew exactly what was wrong with her and were going to give her medicine that would make her all better. She had relief in her eyes. She was finally going to feel better.

John had told me to call him if there was any update on Chantal. I phoned him at work and Thomas at home and gave them both the good news. They were both relieved and very grateful. Within a week of taking the new medication, Chantal had only a few visible spots left. Her temperature was back to normal. She had her appetite back, and she felt so much better. We had our sweet little Chantal back.

During Chantal's stays at the hospital—and there were many—she would help the other little children on the ward. Like Chantal, these children would spend days in the hospital for various reasons. The parents of these children were not always able to be there. Chantal would take the time to keep them company. She played games with them, coloured, painted, and helped them do puzzles. The hospital had this little red car; a child would sit in it, and Chantal would push them around the ward. Even at the age of five, Chantal knew how to make these children happy and also make their stay at the hospital away from their family more bearable.

There was one instance when a small boy, a year old, was sitting in a high chair in front of the nurses' station, waiting to be fed. My daughter, only five years old at the time, asked his mother if she could feed him. The mother gave her permission. Chantal fed the little boy a spoon of cereal. He took it and ate it without a fuss. It was as though the baby and she understood each other, with some kind of communication that only children could understand. Her doctor happened to be doing the rounds on the ward that morning. When he saw Chantal giving the little baby his breakfast, he was amazed. He came up to me with a big smile on his face and said, "She will be a caregiver someday," and that is exactly what she became.

Throughout this time, we benefited from the love and encouragement of our family and friends. Additionally, the hospital had a support group for families to attend. I found sharing our experiences with another was very helpful. They were like another family to me. It made it easier for all of us to cope on a daily basis. Because many of us spent our days in the hospital with our children, we became very close. It was the one-on-one support and the emotions we shared over coffee that made it easier for us to manage.

My husband attended on a few occasions, but the fact that the meetings were held during the weekday made it difficult. This illness caused a financial strain on us, and John had to go to work. I only wished my son and husband could have attended those meetings, as the two seemed to be barely coping. It was still difficult for Thomas and his dad to talk about their feelings.

I recommend support groups to anyone going through a crisis. For me, being able to speak out and share what I was feeling was a great healing. For Thomas and John, it was more difficult.

Throughout the two years, there were many tests done. Bone scans, to check the density of her bones. Echocardiogram to investigate the actions of the heart. The MRI to monitor Chantal's tumor. The tumor was indeed shrinking, which gave us hope that everything was going to be okay. Summer flew right by. Chantal's last few treatment went well. By September the worst seemed to be over. The side effects of the treatments were bearable. We had no more major setbacks. I decided to enroll Chantal back in school. She was going into grade one. The last few treatments were scheduled at the end of the week; therefore, Chantal would miss only a few days of school. She loved school and her grades were good. She was so glad to be able to see her classmates once again.

November 8, 1988, Chantal was admitted to the hospital for her last treatment. We had been looking forward to this moment for over two years. Chantal was doing well. We thanked God that there were no more serious side effects. We were thrilled. The worst was over. We could all breathe a little easier now.

Chantal's clinic visit was scheduled the following week. This time John came with me. The nurse called us into the examining room. We waited patiently for the doctor to arrive. The oncologist walked in the room and asked "How is everyone doing?"

We all said, "Great! We are so happy Chantal's treatments are over."

"Yes, that must be a great feeling. Chantal's blood work has come back normal; that's great news. I will schedule her for another MRI. Chantal has been doing so well, we anticipate the scan to be clear. I will personally call you with the results. Unless you are concerned about something, Chantal's clinic visits will be scheduled for once a month the first year. Then every six months for two years, and then once a year for two years after that. Chantal will have to keep her Hickman in for a few more months."

John and I thanked him for all the care and devotion he gave Chantal during this difficult time. We were so grateful. On the way home for the first time we felt such peace and happiness. Our nightmare was over.

The day of the scan I felt a little nervous. The previous scans showed the tumor shrinking considerably, but this final one was going to be a big factor in Chantal's future. I kept repeating in my head what the doctor had said: "We anticipate the scan to be clear." We decided to leave a little earlier. It had snowed overnight and the roads were covered in snow. We did not want to be late for the MRI. The drivers were being more cautious, so the traffic was a little heavier. We did manage to arrive in plenty of time. We sat there patiently waiting for our turn. It was nerve-racking. Finally, the nurse came and took Chantal by the hand. We gave her a big hug and a kiss and told her we would be here waiting for her. About forty minutes later it was over. Chantal came out of the room, we thanked the nurse, and we all headed for home.

John and I tried to stay positive that everything was going to work out. The tumor had been shrinking all along. Why not now? We went about our same routine around the house. We did not expect the call to be that day. I figured it would be the next day. Before I went to bed and the next morning, I prayed to God that the tumor would be completely gone.

Thomas had gone to work. John and I kept ourselves busy around the house. Every time the phone rang, we jumped. In those days we did not have call display, so we had no idea who was calling. We wanted this moment to be over; however, we did have a sense of relief when it wasn't the doctor on the other end. Around five o'clock the phone rang. John and I were sitting in the family room. I ran to the phone. I picked it up and said, "Hello." I could feel my heart pounding in my chest. My knees were shaking.

The voice on the other end said, "Mrs. Commerford this is Chantal's doctor. I have wonderful news. Chantal's MRI was clear. The tumor is no longer there."

I started to cry. I was so excited I could hardly speak. "Oh, doctor, that is great news, thank you so much."

"You are welcome. Make an appointment next week with the clinic for a follow-up visit."

"I will."

I got off the phone and said, "The tumor is all gone. Thank you, God!"

John had tears in his eyes. "What great news. Chantal the lump on your back is all gone. You are all better now. No more treatments."

She was so happy; I could see she was relieved. We were all so excited. We couldn't wait for Thomas to come home so he could share in the excitement.

A few hours later Thomas walked in. Chantal wanted to be the one to tell her brother the wonderful news. "Thomas, my lump is all gone. I'm all better now."

"That's wonderful, Chantal. I'm so happy for you." He walked towards her and gave her the biggest hug.

We received wonderful news that day, plus Chantal was going to turn seven in a few weeks. It was a wonderful time for celebration. We had a party for Chantal and invited family and friends over to rejoice in this victory. Once again God had answered my prayers.

It was now January 1989; Chantal was a happy seven-year old. She was putting on more weight. Her hair was growing back. She had her wonderful appetite back. I admit it: because of what she had gone through, we did spoil her more than usual. But it was wonderful watching her enjoy herself. On January 11, Chantal's Hickman was removed. During the month of February and again in May, all of Chantal's scans came back clear. The life-threatening disease that inhabited our daughter's body was no longer a part of her. It was now time for our family to return to a normal life.

Chantal was doing great. Her dad and I decided to send her to Camp Quality, a camp established for children with cancer, for one week in August. The camp is located in the southern part of Ontario about four hours from our home. It is in a wooded area with lots of trees, plenty of grassy area for the children to run around. It has a lake for swimming or canoeing. There is a huge recreation hall where they gather for meals and entertainment. There are separate dormitories for girls and boys. The children can play volleyball, learn archery, rappelling, and fishing. They can go on a hot air balloon ride, do crafts, and do so much more. Each child is assigned an adult companion who volunteers their time that week to spend every minute of the day with the child. This is a place where the children do not think of their illness. They simply enjoy being there with friends. Chantal met people who experienced much of what she had.

I remember one summer. It was the last day of camp. John and I went to pick her up. The camp had a huge barbecue for all the parents and siblings. John and I arrived a little early. We didn't see Chantal anywhere. We asked if anybody knew where she was. The person told us Chantal had gone rappelling and for us to follow this certain route that would take us right there. I had no idea what rappelling was. When I saw her strapped in a harness wearing a helmet and climbing from tree to tree, I almost died. I could not believe my little Chantal was brave enough to do this. She was only seven or eight years old. I was so proud of her. We had to take her picture to show her brother and the family. Chantal loved Camp Quality; she always looked forward to the following year. She attended camp as a camper for twelve years.

For the next few years, Chantal remained healthy. During her treatments there was a lot of tension and strain on our marriage. We tried to cope the best way we knew how. Keeping our feelings and emotions bottled up inside certainly did not help the situation, and we became more distant.

When a child is diagnosed with an illness, it is traumatic for the whole family. You fear the unknown. You have financial stress. You may resent your spouse for their lack of support. The tension and anger build. Just as an illness can make some of us stronger and some of us weaker, your marriage will become stronger or weaker as well. In our case, these feelings got the better of us, and my husband and I separated. I know now that it was no one's fault, but at the time our emotions did not make us think in a rational way. We took all our anger and fear out on each other, and it was not healthy. Yes, we had other problems before all of this happened, so I am not putting all the blame on Chantal's illness. It simply did not help. In April 1991, after twenty-two years of marriage, John and I decided to separate. Chantal was nine years old, and Thomas was twenty.

We have since divorced and were able to bring closure by forgiving each other for any wrongs we had done to each other. We each took responsibility for our own actions and to this day we remain friends.

Since Chantal was in remission, I had returned to work full-time. I had my children to keep me company, my job to keep me busy, but I needed something just for me. In June

1992, I decided to join a singles group, not necessarily to meet someone but to socialize. This group was exactly what I needed. There were various activities throughout the month, such as bowling, billiards, games nights, theatre, barbecues, and dinner meetings, and my favourite was going out dancing. You just picked the one you liked the most. I liked the group so much that in the fall of that year, I signed up to become the membership person. My job was to speak to possible new members, tell them about the club, and send them an application to join. Through this group, I made wonderful friends, male and female.

In December I had organized a sleigh ride for the group. A lady named Val called me requesting information about the club and this particular event. I explained to Val what the club represented and all the different activities. I recommended she try one event to see how she liked it, then decide whether or not to join. She decided to come out for the sleigh ride. I told her I was looking forward to meeting her.

I had told everyone to meet at a certain spot. When I arrived a lady approached me and introduced herself as Val. She was a very pretty lady, five feet six inches tall, slim, with dark curly hair. Val looked rather nervous, which was understandable. I knew when I went out on my own for the first time, it was pretty scary, so I could relate to Val being a little apprehensive. I welcomed her to the event and introduced her to everyone.

It was freezing cold that night, and due to lack of snow we ended up having a hay ride. We all enjoyed the evening. After the ride I invited everyone over to the house for hot chocolate. Val and I hit it off right away. We became close friends. The spring and summer of 1993, Val and I became even closer. We were inseparable. We attended many of the activities throughout the month. Going out dancing was our favourite.

By September, Chantal remained healthy and was going into grade five. Val and I were out dancing. I happened to look over and saw this man sitting at another table. He was very handsome, tall, well dressed. He had grey hair, a black mustache, and a wonderful smile. I couldn't keep my eyes off him. I felt a very strong connection with this person. I couldn't explain it. I knew I had to meet this man. I wanted to ask him to dance; unfortunately, he was not alone, and I did not want to interfere. The whole evening I kept looking his way. As we were leaving the hall, they happened to be leaving at the same time. I spoke, wishing them a good night. It was he who replied, "You too."

I told Val there was something about this man, and I wanted to know more about him. As it turns out, he had just met the girl he was with that night, and the following week I saw him again. One of the ladies from our club came up to me and told me there was somebody who was interested in getting information about the club. It was he. I was so excited. I knew this was my chance to finally get to know him.

I went up to him and said, "Hi, my name is Louise. I'm in charge of membership for the club. I hear you are interested in knowing more about the group."

"Hello, I am Alain and yes, I would like some information."

65

I noticed he had an attractive French accent. Being French myself, I knew that was a great advantage. I invited him to sit at our table and introduced him to some of the members. I explained some of the details regarding the club. I told him we went dancing every Wednesday and Saturday night. He seemed very interested. Alain gave me his address. I told him I would mail him the application the next day. He thanked me, and then I asked him to dance. Alain and I danced together most of the evening. At the end of the night, he walked Val and me to our car. "Good-night. See you next week." We both said good-night. I couldn't wait until the following week.

For the next three weeks, Alain would be sitting at our usual table, waiting for Val and me to arrive. I was really hoping he would ask me out. That day I thought to myself, *If he doesn't ask me to go out soon, I will ask him.* That very night, before the dance, Alain called me at home and asked me out for dinner on Friday night. He also asked if he could pick me up and take me to the dance, since we were both going to the same place. Of course, I agreed to both. Alain and I enjoyed all of our time together. He too loved to go to the dances. Even the nights we stayed in and watched a movie were exciting to me. He was so sweet and gentle.

Alain happened to be in the navy; this was the reason he came to St. Catharines. The military had two naval ships that needed repair, and the dry dock here in the city had received the contract for the repairs. Alain was one of the officers doing the quality inspections on the repairs. You can call it fate. I believe Alain came here for a reason, and that was for us to be together. I truly believe that.

It was November, and Alain and I had been dating a little over two months. My daughter was going to have her eleventh birthday. I was planning a party for her, with eight little girlfriends. Unfortunately, I ended up scheduled to work that Saturday. It was only a four-hour shift; since we always worked alone, I couldn't trade with anyone else. Rather than change her party, Alain surprised me by volunteering to supervise. I don't know many men who would take this on. But Alain, being the man he was, decided he wanted to do this for my daughter and me. I asked my daughter if that was okay with her, and she agreed.

So that day I had all the preparations ready for her birthday. The only thing Alain had to do was keep an eye out. I called to see how things were going making sure the girls weren't driving him crazy. I needn't have worried. They were playing musical chairs, and Alain was in charge of stopping the music. The party was a success, and everyone was happy. This man always went out of his way to look after my family. That was very important to me. It did not take long before my family became his. In March of 1994, we decided to move in together. Alain loved my children, and he was wonderful with them. Fortunately, they loved Alain the same way I did, and I knew this was going to be a happy, healthy relationship.

Being in the military, Alain was shipped to different parts of the world. At the time we met, he only had a year and a half remaining in my home town. In August of '94 he was going to be sent to another post in British Columbia. As much as I was committed to this relationship, quitting my job and uprooting my children to move three thousand miles to another part of the world was a big change. However, it did not take long for me to realize I would go anywhere to be with him. When we both realized how much we loved each other, Alain asked to be stationed close by and in the same province. We were lucky, if you think luck has anything to do with this. The military complied, and in a year and half his next posting would be in Windsor, Ontario, four hours away.

Being a family again was a wonderful feeling. We all got along so well. Alain and I continued to go to the dances. In July of 1994 Alain took Chantal and me to St. Petersburg, Florida. It gave Alain a chance to visit with his mom. I had met Jacqueline before Alain and I dated. She had come to St. Catharines to visit her son. He brought her to one of our dances. I thought she was a new prospect for the club. That night I saw where Alain inherited all of his wonderful qualities. Our time in Florida would give us the opportunity to get to know each other even more, and she would also get to know my daughter.

Jacqueline is the sweetest, most loving person you could ever meet. She treated Chantal and me with such kindness. My daughter and I both got to know her, and I fell in love with her as quickly as I fell in love with her son. During that week we spent a day at Disney World, and the rest of the week Chantal spent in the pool. I had signed her up for swimming lessons months before. They really paid off that week. She was like a fish in water. We had a wonderful, memorable trip that week.

Chantal was enjoying her teen years. Thomas was now twenty-two years old, working steady, and living in his own apartment. Our first Christmas together as a family was so memorable. Alain got to know my side of the family a little better. The following months flew by quickly. Chantal was doing well in school, and the summer was just around the corner. I was counting the remaining weeks before Alain had to leave for Windsor.

In August it was a beautiful Sunday afternoon. Alain was packing and getting ready to move to Windsor for his new posting. Watching him pack was very difficult for me. I dreaded this moment. I thought I was prepared, but I guess I wasn't. It was time for Alain to leave. We held each other for a long time. He kissed Chantal and me and told us he loved us. Alain picked up his suitcase and said, "I will call you as soon as I get there." Chantal and I told him we loved him and to have a safe trip. We waved good-bye one last time as he drove off. I tried to keep busy the rest of the day, but my thoughts were on Alain, and I would cry. Four hours later the phone rang; it was Alain. Hearing his voice on the other end of the phone saying he had arrived safely and telling me how much he loved me brought me comfort.

Because of his job Alain would be allowed to come home only every second weekend. I really missed him the times we were apart. He would always leave after supper on Sunday night. Chantal and I always got a big kiss and a hug before he left. I would watch him as he walked towards his car. Alain would turn and wave a final good-bye. It broke my heart to see him leave. When I could no longer see the car, I would always go upstairs to my room and cry. I tried not to cry in front of my daughter, but she knew. The following visit Chantal told Alain how sad I was after he left. He told me he felt bad leaving me; unfortunately, it could not be helped.

Alain continued to drive back and forth for the first year. For Chantal and me, life continued. I kept busy working. Chantal was in grade six and enjoying school with her friends. Since her chemotherapy she had remained very healthy. In the spring of 1995, Chantal had a cold. This was unusual for her. She rarely had colds. Now, for some reason, she would get over one cold and a few weeks later have another. I thought this strange, but also that school and contact with other kids meant that germs spread.

It was a Thursday in early April, a beautiful sunny afternoon. I wasn't working that day. Chantal was playing in her room. I had invited my friend Val over for a visit. We were both sitting in the living room talking and drinking our coffee. All of a sudden Chantal decided to come down to tell me she had been having some difficulty breathing. My heart started to pound. I asked her to explain what she meant.

Chantal explained, "Since my last cold, once in a while I find it more difficult to catch my breath."

I was furious. "What do you mean by difficulty catching your breath?"

"I just find it harder to breathe."

"Why didn't you say something to me before this?"

"I don't know. It doesn't happen all the time. I thought it was because of my cold."

I took a deep breath to calm myself. I did not want her to see me upset. I immediately got up to call her doctor. He was very understanding. He told me to take Chantal to the hospital for an X-ray. He would call them to let them know I was coming. Then I was to return with the image to his office so he could review it. Val looked as concerned as I was. I told her I would call her as soon as I had more news. We hugged each other, and Chantal and I left for the hospital.

The doctor, after viewing the X-ray, said, "I see a lesion in the chest. I suggest you take Chantal back to the hospital in Hamilton for further testing. I will call the clinic and make an appointment for you."

I had a gnawing feeling in my stomach and a lump in my throat. I tried to stay positive. I tried hard. But all I could think about was that Chantal's cancer was back. I wondered what was going on in her mind. On the drive home, instead of me telling my daughter things were going to be fine, Chantal said to me, "Mom, stop worrying. Everything is going to be all right." Even at twelve years old, Chantal showed no fear. Seeing her so brave gave me some encouragement.

When we returned home, I noticed my son's car in the parking lot. Chantal decided she was going over to a friend's house to play. Thomas told me he just stopped in for a few minutes on his way to work. I waited for Chantal to leave and proceeded to tell Thomas what happenèd. He looked very upset. He didn't know what to say. I hated the fact he had to leave for work. "I will call you tomorrow from the hospital as soon as I know more."

We hugged and he left. I still needed to release some of this anxiety I was feeling. I ran to the bedroom, threw myself onto the pillow, and began to sob. I began to pray. "God, you have always been there for me. Please look after us and give us the strength to get through this." After a few minutes of feeling sorry for myself, I felt peace.

I had to phone Alain in Windsor and tell him the news. He told me he loved me and was on his way home. I then called Val and told her the same. It normally took four hours to drive from Windsor to St. Catharines. I don't know how it happened, but Alain arrived at the house in just a little over three hours. I was so happy to see him. I always felt safe around Alain. I know Chantal felt the same. That night Alain and I held each other and tried to stay positive.

Our appointment was scheduled for nine o'clock that Friday morning. Remembering the past, I packed a bag for Chantal, just in case she would have to stay in the hospital. We woke up around seven o'clock. We were all too nervous to eat. We figured when we got hungry we would grab something at the hospital. It had been almost two years since Chantal and I were at this hospital. This was the first time for Alain. Seeing it again brought back memories, many I chose not to remember.

We went right to the clinic. The secretary told us to go to the first floor have an X-ray taken and bring it back with us. Thank God we didn't have to wait long. We rushed back to the clinic. We now had to wait our turn. It was nerve-racking. I found trying to keep my thoughts positive was difficult especially now. Waiting for our turn seemed to take forever. We then heard "Chantal Commerford." We stood up and followed the nurse to the examining room. Again we had to wait. Finally the door swung open, and there was her oncologist.

"Sorry to keep you waiting. I have examined the X-ray, and the lesions Chantal's doctor saw are actually scar tissue from her biopsy. There is some fluid on the lungs. I will give you a prescription for antibiotics. She will have to take the pills for ten days. Before you leave the clinic, schedule an appointment to come back once the pills are finished. You are then free to go home." We were ecstatic. We thanked the doctor, made the appointment, and left.

We could all breathe a sigh of relief. It was wonderful news. As soon as we got home, I called Thomas and Val to give them the update. Chantal's dad had moved four hours away because of his job. I felt I needed to call him and let him know what was happening. He thanked me for calling him. He was happy and relieved it wasn't serious.

Alain and I were on holidays for the next two weeks. The antibiotics seemed to be working, as Chantal no longer experienced breathing problems. On Tuesday I received a call from the doctor in Hamilton telling me that they had similar cases with other children, who experienced breathing difficulties. There was a meeting with the parents at the hospital on Thursday. I told him we would be there. *Is this cause for me to worry?* I tried to dismiss this thought. I told Alain about the meeting. He saw the worried look on my face and said,

"Louise, let's just see what they have to tell us. Let's not assume the worst."

At the meeting, I recognized many of the parents. We had spent many days supporting one another at the hospital. Here we were once again. The room was small but large enough to seat all of us comfortably. At the front stood a long desk directly before a blackboard. A slide projector was on the corner of the desk. Four chairs were placed beside the desk for each doctor. Of the four in the room, only one was a doctor for Chantal. They introduced themselves and then began to explain to us their discovery. I had brought a pad and pen to write down all the information we received.

I found keeping a personal journal with my thoughts and feelings and a medical journal with dates, times, doctors, drugs used, and side effects during Chantal's illness was really important, especially when it came to answering questions. The answer would be right there in front of me. I wouldn't have to try and think about it.

One of the doctors spoke. "Through further investigation, we found that one of the drugs in your child's protocol, Adriamycin, had side effects which caused damage to different organs." In Chantal's case, it was her heart. She now had mitral valve regurgitation. The drug had damaged the lower part of her heart, causing the mitral valve to remain slightly open and to leak. Hearing those words made me sick to my stomach. I couldn't believe it. All I wanted to do was leave the room and cry. After fighting cancer, Chantal, at the age of thirteen, would have to face heart disease. How on earth were we going to explain this to her? The doctor gave each parent the name of the specialist who was to look after our child. We were to make an appointment as soon as possible. Chantal would now have to be in the care of a cardiologist.

CHAPTER 4

Facing Heart Disease

C hantal would have to be put on drugs to control her blood pressure and her leaky valve. We were about to face another nightmare. I thought I had seen the last of this hospital. This news was devastating to both Alain and me. On the way to the car, I said, "Alain how are we going to tell Chantal?"

I remember him saying, "We will explain to her exactly what the doctors told us. Louise, Chantal is strong; she will get through this. We all will." Alain always seemed to know what to say to make me feel better.

All the way home I prayed to God for strength and courage for Chantal and the family. As I opened the front door, Chantal was right there waiting for us. We sat down on the couch and proceeded to tell her what the doctors had told us. I was shocked by her reaction. It was as if she knew. Once again my beautiful daughter showed her courage and strength. She never complained, never showed fear. She simply went along with everything we told her, as though it was meant to be. She not only fought her cancer, but now she had to face heart disease.

All we could do was stand by her, support her, and try to stay positive. God answered my prayers. Seeing my daughter show such courage gave me the strength and courage to get through this ordeal. We told her she was a brave little girl, that we loved her very much. Alain and I decided to hold off telling her brother and her dad until we spoke to the cardiologist and knew all the facts.

First thing Friday morning I called the doctor's office. The appointment was scheduled for the following Tuesday morning. The nurse told us to go directly to the second floor, have an electrocardiogram and echocardiogram taken, then come to the appointment. Their office was directly across the hall. The electrocardiogram, or EKG, records the heartbeat and the electrical activities of the heart. The echocardiogram shows the internal structure of the heart and how the blood flows through it. The nurse told me it would take about an hour. Both tests were done, and then it was time to see the cardiologist.

The oncologist had talked to the heart specialist, so she knew about Chantal's case. The cardiologist examined Chantal and, after looking at the tests, explained that Chantal's bicuspid valve, which is the mitral valve situated between the left atrium and the left ventricle, was damaged. That lower part of the heart was damaged by the drug, causing the mitral valve to remain slightly opened and leak blood. After hearing this I felt numb. I knew I had no control of the situation. The only thing I could do was put my trust in God and the doctor to look after Chantal.

My next question to the doctor was, "Will Chantal need to have a heart transplant?"

"I don't feel it is necessary at this time. It is too soon to tell. Chantal will be put on blood thinners and medication to stabilize her heart. I would like to see Chantal in a few weeks to see how the medication is working."

We thanked her and left to get Chantal's prescription filled. On the way home Chantal said to me, "Mom, I'm glad you asked the doctor about the transplant, because that has been on my mind all week." "Chantal, the doctor did tell us it was too soon to worry about that right now."

Having faith in God, I trusted he would take care of my family. I always communicate with God directly. I speak to God the same way I speak to you. It brings me peace. At that time, however, with Chantal going through another illness, I was starting to have doubts. *When is this all going to end?* I asked of God. My daughter was the one going through all of this, and I was the one feeling sorry for myself. I wanted to know why this was happening. I hated every bit of it. I wanted it to go away.

Having negative thoughts and losing faith is a normal reaction when your child is sick and you have no control over the situation. It is fear that brings on this emotional state. That is okay. Never be afraid to show your true feelings. Keeping your emotions bottled up inside you will only make it worse. Don't be afraid to have a one-on-one conversation with God, He understands what you are going through. God will bring you light during your darkest times.

The next few months Chantal no longer experienced breathing difficulties. Everything was going great. Chantal was doing fine. In June she graduated to grade seven. In the beginning her visits to the cardiologist were every six weeks. Meanwhile, Alain was still travelling back and forth. I really wanted to be near him. We were so in love, and we missed being near each other. After giving it serious consideration, in August of 1995 I decided to quit my job of twenty-two years and move with my daughter to Windsor to live with Alain. Thomas was twenty-four years old at the time and, as he was working, chose to stay behind.

There were only two years left in Alain's contract with the military, only two more years in Windsor before he could officially retire from the navy. Even though I was going to Windsor for only two years, it was very difficult to leave my son. I had never been away from him before. It was a sad moment in my life when I had to say good-bye. With tears in our eyes, we all hugged and kissed. I told Thomas we were only four hours away and that we would come to visit as often as possible. He was sad to see us leave. I called Thomas the minute we arrived in Windsor. I told him I loved him and that we would see him as soon as we were all settled in. Alain had taken care of all the arrangements and found us a place near Chantal's new school. It did not take long before Chantal, Alain, and I were all settled into our new home.

While Chantal was happy to be part of a family once again, she was apprehensive regarding her first day at a new school. I reminded Chantal that it was always easy for her to make friends, but for some reason she was still nervous. The night before school I told her I would go with her to see the principal. She seemed a little less stressed. The next morning we both walked into the principal's office and introduced ourselves. He was very compassionate towards Chantal, telling her that he was personally going to introduce her to her teacher and new classmates. Chantal was relieved, to say the least. I thanked him for looking after Chantal. We hugged and I told her to have a good day. I knew that everything was going to be okay.

We did not live far from the school, which allowed Chantal to come home for lunch. I couldn't wait to see her and ask her how her first morning went. At lunchtime I heard the back door open. "Mom, look what I have." She showed me a piece of paper with the names and phone numbers of the girls in her class.

"That's wonderful, dear. I am so happy for you. I told you the kids would like you." She had such a wonderful personality. How could people not want to be her friend?

"All of my new friends live close by, so we will be able to play together."

"I told you everything was going to be fine."

She told me the principal introduced her to the class, and all the children welcomed her. She was so excited she could hardly eat her lunch. She just wanted to get back to school. That year we had plenty of sleepovers and after-school get-togethers. What she lacked during her younger years because of her illness she certainly made up for during her teens.

It was a wonderful year for Chantal. She was feeling great and having lots of fun with her new friends. The following spring was her confirmation. We decided to have a little party.

I invited her dad, his new girlfriend, and her brother, her uncle Sandy and aunt Ginette, whom Chantal had asked to be her sponsor. It was great seeing everyone, especially my son. I really missed him. Chantal was also very happy to see her family. We had a great time.

The school year was coming to an end. It was time for graduation. When I was in grade eight, all we had were a few goodies the teacher brought in on the last day of school. These young girls were talking limousine and fancy dresses. Chantal was so petite that it was difficult to find her a party dress. I had one made of black satin. She looked beautiful. The parents did, however, veto the limousine. Chantal had done very well in school. At the graduation she was presented with two awards, one for English and one for French. We were very proud of her.

Alain's leave was extended another year, which meant we had to remain in Windsor for an extra year. Chantal was entering high school. Her health was good, which was very encouraging. Chantal's visits to the cardiologist were now scheduled every six months. Alain and I didn't feel the need to change cardiologist. We decided on the day of Chantal's appointment we would drive to Hamilton, then to St. Catharines and visit with Thomas, other family, and friends.

Chantal's check-ups were always good news. She was feeling great, had plenty of energy. She had a wonderful appetite; she weighed seventy-five pounds. She was having the time of her life with her friends. Even with her heart problems, Chantal was able to lead a normal life.

Every summer Chantal attended camp, where she enjoyed all the wonderful activities provided to keep the children happy and busy. Her favourite was doing crafts. Even at a young age, she was very artistic. She loved making things with her own hands. She made beaded bracelets and painted T-shirts and sneakers. One summer she made us a beautiful wooden mailbox, which I have hanging by my side door. The year Canada changed our dollar bill to a Loonie, she made a wooden bank in the shape of a loon. Chantal was a camper for twelve years, and every year she came home with something special she had made with her own two hands.

Chantal really treasured that week. For this time, worries and illness were not part of their lives. Only wonderful memories, pleasant and happy moments, featured in the experience. The children and the activities were not the only thing that Chantal looked forward to. What really meant a lot to her was sharing every minute of every day with her companion. She was always very fortunate to be paired off with someone she loved to spend her time with. Chantal deserved it, after everything she had gone through.

Jennifer was the one companion who especially stood out. She was not much taller than Chantal. She had short blonde hair and a beautiful smile. She was like a big sister to Chantal. She was very loving and caring towards my daughter. Over the years they became very close, spending time together not only at camp but outside as well. Jennifer would come to St. Catharines and take Chantal out for the day, or we would drive Chantal to Jennifer's for the weekend. They shared many feelings and memories, which meant a great deal to Chantal. In fact, Chantal was there when Jennifer met her husband, John, another volunteer at camp. When the two of them fell in love and married, Chantal was a bridesmaid in their wedding. At that time Chantal was sixteen years old. I was so proud of the young lady Chantal had become.

At the age of six, enjoying a day at camp

Chantal, age twelve, relaxing at camp

Grade eight graduation, thirteen years old

Bridesmaid at her companion Jennifer's
wedding, sixteen years old

I was a stay-at-home mom during those three years in Windsor. I found it very difficult to make friends there. I even took an evening class, hoping to meet new people. It just didn't work out. The only socializing Alain and I did was playing euchre on Friday nights at the military base. I enjoyed those evenings but couldn't wait to move back to St. Catharines. Chantal had completed grade ten at high school and was having a wonderful social life with her friends. Alain's service in the navy was coming to an end.

On June 15, 1998, Alain was officially discharged from the military. All our friends and family lived in my home town. I yearned to go back home to be with all of them, especially Thomas, whom I missed dearly. Alain was too young to completely retire; we knew he would have to find a new job. My husband applied for jobs in our area and, because of his skills, was able to find employment quickly. Even though Chantal was upset because she had to leave her Windsor friends, she was still happy to be back with her old friends. We returned to St. Catharines in July of 1998, where it did not take long for all of us to settle into our new home.

Chantal was looking forward to August for her week at camp. I had found a part-time job at a local retail store. Alain was enjoying his new job, and the three of us were simply content to be back where we belonged. My son was close to us, and we were near family and friends. After being back in St. Catharines for a few years, our lives were more stable, and Alain and I decided it was time to get married. After living together for six years, we were going to make it official. Alain and I had a wonderful relationship. I knew this was the right thing to do. I never regretted being with this man. We set the date for October 7, 2000. Chantal helped me make plans for the wedding. It was an honour having my son Thomas walk me down the aisle and to have Chantal as my maid of honour. At that moment I was so very proud of both my children. I have a wonderful video of my daughter dancing at my wedding. She never sat down for a minute. Seeing her with such energy was a miracle.

Chantal's health remained stable, which enabled her to complete another three years of high school, graduating from grade thirteen. During Chantal's three years at her new school, she signed up to be a cheerleader. The girls would form a pyramid, and because Chantal was so petite, she was always the one at the peak. She assisted the teacher in a class for students with special needs. She showed so much compassion for these special kids. She enjoyed working with them, and they in turn loved her.

I remember Chantal telling me how she helped a student at school who had Tourette syndrome. She happened to be sick one day, so the boy refused to do his work on the computer. The teacher asked him why he wouldn't do it. His reply was, "Chantal's not here to help me, so I'm not doing it." The teacher was surprised to hear this. The next day she told Chantal what had happened. She was very flattered but had to tell him that if she was not at school, he still had to do his work. Another year Chantal helped a boy with Down syndrome. She came home one day with this letter he wrote saying how much he loved her and would she be his girlfriend. She said to me, "Mom, what do I say to him? I don't want to hurt his feelings." I told her to tell him she was sorry, but she already had a boyfriend. It was not true, but that was the only way she could let him down gently. He understood. The love, compassion, and caring Chantal showed in those three years at that high school was felt by many. In June 2000, at her grade thirteen graduation, Chantal received the Humanitarian Award. She was seventeen years old. What a proud day that was for our family.

My daughter made friends with many people, especially one close friend. Alissa is a beautiful girl who stands about five inches taller than Chantal. She has long blonde hair, fair skin, and a beautiful smile. The two of them were inseparable. They spent the days at school and many evenings together. Alissa's parents loved having Chantal in their home. This was a second home to her. I never had to ask her where she was going. It was always, "See ya later, Mom, I'm going over to Alissa's." Their relationship was very special. They seem to complement each other. When one was down the other would know how to make the other feel better. Certainly, there were times they ticked each other off. Like everyone else, they had their disagreements, but they always took the time to work it out. They stood by each other during the good times and the bad. They always respected each other. This is the love that Alissa and Chantal shared as friends.

During the summer Chantal was involved with rowing. Some of her friends were on a rowing team and asked her to be their coxswain. That is the person at the front of the boat giving directions. Chantal always had a good set of lungs, and because of her small frame she was perfect for the job.

Eventually my daughter found part-time work at a local supermarket, working as a cashier. There she met some wonderful co-workers and got along with everyone. While she had her licence to drive, there were times when I had to pick her up after work. She would tell me to come at a certain time, and I would be waiting in the car, watching her help the others clean up after their shift. The girls appreciated this and loved working with her. Chantal always felt the need to help others. So we agreed that on the nights I would pick her up, I would come fifteen minutes later than the end of her shift. That way if she wanted to help out, I wouldn't have to wait.

Chantal was always able to connect with people of different ages, young or old. There was one lady in particular, Cathy, who worked with her at the supermarket. Cathy was in her fifties, was five feet six inches tall, had short brown hair, and wore glasses. Cathy and Chantal really hit it off. Chantal would often go over to her house to play cards and have many laughs together. I found out later there were certain things Chantal shared with Cathy that she felt she could not share with me. Today I understand why. Cathy was not only a friend but like a second mom to Chantal. Chantal knew Cathy would never break that trust. My daughter and I loved to go out for dinner; I would ask Chantal if she wanted to go for supper, and she would say, "Can't, Mom, I'm going to Cathy's." There were times I felt a little rejected.

My husband and I once had a family barbecue. I really wanted to meet this lady, so I asked Chantal to invite her. She introduced us, and by the end of the night I could see what my daughter saw in her. Even though Cathy was my age, I could see how well they communicated. She is a great person. They had developed a wonderful friendship. After meeting Cathy, I no longer felt intimidated. Thanks to my daughter, to this day Cathy and I are good friends.

Chantal's heart condition never became a threat. She continued her medication, and her check-ups at the hospital were always good news. August of 2000 was to be Chantal's last summer as a camper. Chantal was going to turn eighteen years old that November, and once you reach that age, you can no longer be a camper. Because of who she was, Chantal continued her involvement with the camp; she wanted to give back what she received. The following summer, at the age of eighteen, Chantal became a companion to a young camper. For the whole week, it was her turn to dedicate herself to a child, spending every minute of every day making a life happier. She understood everything that child felt, because she had experienced it all herself.

When you can relate to what other people have experienced, it can make you more compassionate, more caring, more understanding, and more loving towards them. This came naturally to Chantal.

It was September of 2000, time for Chantal to move on to university. Since the beginning of high school, Chantal knew exactly what career path to take. She wanted to work with children or adults with speech and communication disorders. Chantal applied at our local university. It is a wonderful school, and because Chantal's marks were excellent, she was accepted. She wanted to apply out of town to experience living away from home, but for financial reasons and doctor's appointments, we decided against that idea. For my own selfish aims, I wanted Chantal close to home.

Throughout those four years at university, Chantal remained healthy. She continued to work at the grocery store, hung out with her friends, and looked forward to her weeks at camp. In April of 2005, after completing her four years of university, Chantal received with honours her B.A. in linguistics. Sitting in the auditorium that day, I thought of all Chantal had endured throughout her years. I watched her as she went up on the stage. As the dean reached out to hand her the diploma, I saw the beautiful young woman she had become. This brought tears to my eyes. My daughter had worked so hard to accomplish her goals, her desires. That afternoon she had achieved them.

The rest of the summer she continued her part-time job at the grocery store. In August she volunteered her week at Camp Quality as a companion to a camper. Chantal also wanted to study for one more year, in order to specialize in her field. She applied out of town and was accepted. In September of 2005, Chantal was going to be able to experience living away from home. Orillia was approximately four hours away from home. Chantal had searched the internet for a place to live during that year. We went down one Saturday in June to look at all these rentals. We found a five-bedroom home close to the college that rented to students. Chantal was the first to see the place, so she had the first choice of rooms. She decided on taking the full basement, as it had its own washroom and much bigger living space. We found out later that all the girls in the house were going to the same college.

We had bought her a small car to help her get around. The car would enable her to come home for visits or doctor's appointments. We moved Chantal the weekend before school started. We met her roommates, who all seemed very nice. They all got along, so it made her life away from home a pleasant one. Chantal and I talked on the phone quite frequently. Alain and I really missed having her around. Chantal was a great little cook; she always watched the Food Network on television. She loved to experiment with different recipes, and having her cook for us was always a treat. Her dad, Alain, and I would go and visit her as often as possible. We were grateful when the year was over. Chantal would be coming home again to stay. In October 2006 Chantal completed her year, receiving her B.A. in Communication Disorders. Again I watched my beautiful daughter receive yet another diploma. This was another proud moment for our family.

It was now time for Chantal to find employment. She searched diligently on the computer to find work in her field. She applied to several job openings and went to interviews but was never given the opportunity. She decided to go back to her old job at the grocery store until something came up. Life continued for all of us. Thomas, Alain, and I continued to work full-time. There had been no changes in Chantal's condition at that time. She remained healthy. Finally, in January 2007, Chantal's determination paid off. She was hired by the Catholic school board for a six-month contract. Chantal was now able to go out into the workforce and do what she did best: helping and caring for others.

The work took her to different schools in the area, where she taught children with learning disabilities. It enabled her to connect with each child on a personal level, and she loved it. Working with each individual was sometimes heartbreaking for Chantal. She could spend only thirty-five minutes a week with each child. Because she was so compassionate towards each student, she felt this was not enough time. It took some of them fifteen to twenty minutes just to settle down. Once the child was willing to focus, it was time for the class to end. This frustrated Chantal. She felt the need to spend more time with them. Unfortunately, with the funding cutbacks, this was not possible. In June 2007 Chantal's contract with the school board ended. That part of her life's experience was over. It was now time to seek new employment.

Travel was another passion of Chantal's, and in July she was able to plan a Disney cruise with a girlfriend, without her mom and dad. This was her first big trip as an adult. She was so excited. When Chantal first told me about it, I was a little apprehensive. I worried when she went away on her own. All the old fears would come back to haunt me. After her battle with cancer and now dealing with heart disease, I felt the need to have her close to me. Close to her doctors in case of an emergency. She said to me, "Mom, nothing is going to happen to me. I will be okay. I will not live my life worrying about my health. I want to experience all that I can in my life and do what makes me happy." I guess I got told. But, as a mother, I still worried about her, especially when she was going that far from home.

Chantal's dream was always to swim with the dolphins. This trip gave her that opportunity. She had a week filled with wonderful memories. I, on the other hand, was grateful all those swimming lessons came in handy at last. She ended up having the time of her life and returned home safe and sound. This time all of my fears were for nothing.

Upon her return Chantal persevered trying to find full-time work. In September 2007 Chantal's search was over. She was hired as a rehabilitation therapist for a London, Ontario, firm, two hours away. They offered a home program for adults with brain injuries. While Chantal was excited about the work and living on her own, the best part was that she was going to be near her close friend Alissa, who a few years prior to this had moved to London. It was heart-wrenching for my husband and me to see her go. Our daughter had grown into a fine young lady. I knew I would have to cut those apron strings sooner or later, but I had wished that day never came. Alain and I knew this was a part of Chantal's journey, and we needed to support her. We helped her pack her belongings. Thomas and Alain loaded up the truck, and we followed her to London.

Chantal had found herself a nice basement apartment with all the comforts of home. It was a one-bedroom, with kitchen, bathroom, laundry room, and large living room with a fireplace. The couple who owned the house occupied the upstairs. With the landlord living upstairs, Chantal would not be on her own. This gave me a sense of peace. We helped her settle in, and it was time to say good-bye. It was a sad moment when I had to say good-bye to Chantal when she left for school, but I knew then she was coming back. This time she was moving out for good. I held her close to me. I did not want to let her go. We both had tears in our eyes. "Don't worry, Mom, I will be okay. I will come home and visit. You can come visit me anytime." My heart was aching. My little girl was no longer a baby. She was an adult. She wouldn't need me as much anymore. It was time for me to let her spread her wings and fly. Thomas and Alain embraced her and said their good-byes. On the way home I spoke to God and asked him to watch over Chantal.

Two weeks later Chantal had the weekend off, so Alain and I decided to go down and visit. When I walked into her apartment, I noticed a cat sleeping on her chair. I thought it belonged to the landlord. Chantal told me that Alissa, who was thrilled to have her best friend near, adopted the cat to keep her company, making Spencer a housewarming gift. At the time Spencer was a two-year-old short-haired tabby with grey and black markings. A beautiful cat, fully rounded with a great disposition. I knew Chantal loved animals. We had adopted a cat months before she moved. We named him Oliver. He was a black and white four-month-old tabby. Chantal fell in love with Oliver, and he loved being around her. Oliver would always sleep on her bed. Now she had her own cat to love. Chantal and Spencer became good friends in no time.

Chantal loved working with her clients, and they loved her. She showed them incredible compassion and patience. I recall Chantal telling me about one particular incident that happened at her work. A resident was fixated on the same daily routine. Each day they would give him chocolate chip cookies for an afternoon snack. One day one of the other therapists was nearing the end of her shift. She gave him different cookies, because they ran out of the others. He would not eat them, and he kept insisting they give him chocolate chip cookies. The girl tried to explain to him that they did not have the chocolate chip cookies and said to eat the ones she gave him. He went on and on about the cookies, and, like many of us, she lost her patience. He got himself all upset, and the next person coming on shift was Chantal. The girl explained the situation, and Chantal immediately went to see him.

When Chantal saw how agitated her client was, she knew exactly what to do to ease his discomfort. "I know how much you love your chocolate chip cookies, but unfortunately the office has made a mistake and bought the wrong kind. Just try them and see how you like them. I will make sure they give you the right ones tomorrow." She did not tell him to eat the ones he was given. She gave him an option. She spoke to him in a loving, compassionate, soft voice that he could relate to. The frustrated resident agreed to eat the cookies in front of him, but before that, he said to my daughter, "Chantal, you are so nice to me, and you don't get mad at me. I wish everybody was like you." With tears in her eyes, my daughter replied to him, "It is so easy to be nice to you," as she said his name and gave him a big hug. That moment he calmed down and ate the cookies. To him it was a big deal, and Chantal understood that. Because of her gift of understanding and compassion, she was able to make him feel better.

Months went by, and we visited each other when we could. Unfortunately, she worked most weekends and was not always able to be with family over the holidays. Since Chantal had just started this new job, she had to work during Christmas. Being a French Canadian family, we had our biggest celebration on Christmas Eve. That first year, we had Christmas Eve the weekend before, so Chantal could be a part of the festivities. There were employees at Chantal's work who had families of their own, so for the next few years Chantal volunteered to work the holidays, letting them spend time with their loved ones. I always understood why Chantal did this and eventually figured out that it was not the date that was important; it was having everyone around to help celebrate. We continued to celebrate Christmas Eve on a weekend she was not working.

CHAPTER 5

Trip to Jamaica

In January 2008 Chantal had the opportunity to go to Jamaica for a week, with three other friends from camp. She was so excited. When Chantal called me, she told me she was scheduled to leave on Saturday, January 13 and come back on the twentieth. I asked her if she had purchased travelling insurance. With Chantal's medical history, it was important she have extra coverage. She assured me she had. I told her to have a great time and take lots of pictures.

Chantal was now twenty-five years old, and for the last fifteen years, other than when she had the occasional cold, I had stopped worrying about Chantal's well-being. She remained very healthy, considering her condition. One Saturday afternoon around two o'clock, I was sitting and reading while Alain was at work. The phone rang. The voice on the other end of the phone said to me, "Louise, this is Jeremy. I am one of the friends travelling with Chantal. I hate to say this to you, but Chantal has suffered a stroke."

Within seconds all these thoughts were racing through my head. *Oh my God, this can't be happening. Chantal is only twenty-five years old. How can she have a stroke? She is so far away I am not there with her. What am I going to do? She needs me. How are we going to get her home?* I wasn't thinking straight. The more I thought about what Jeremy said, the more my heart sank. I started to feel nauseous. At that moment it was like a bolt of lightning hit me: *Louise, you need to calm down and listen to what Jeremy has to say.* I took a deep breath, sat down, and asked him to explain what happened.

"It's our last day in Jamaica, and we made plans to go see Marley's museum before we left tonight. I told Chantal I would come to her room in the morning and pick her up. When I knocked, Chantal opened the door and collapsed in my arms. I asked her what she felt before this. She told me she had been taking a shower and felt weak and dizzy. I'm a nurse. From the symptoms Chantal described and from the numbness on her right side, I believe she has suffered a stroke. I immediately took her to a hospital."

"The hospital care is not like back home. Chantal is in the hallway lying on a gurney with no blanket and no pillow. They did, however, take a CT head scan when we arrived, and it did not show lesions. They are not telling us much. I've tried to talk to the doctor, but he is busy with other patients. All I can tell you right now is Chantal is not able to travel. She is coherent and able to talk to us. She is trying to stay strong, and she's happy we are with her. I assure you we will not leave her side.

One of our friends travelling with us went back to the hotel to borrow a pillow and blanket to make her more comfortable."

All I could visualize was my daughter lying on a cold gurney with nothing to keep her warm. My heart sank even more. I just wanted her home. "Please thank him for me."

I couldn't imagine what Chantal was going through. She was so far from home. I did not know if we would have to go to Jamaica to bring her back or, God forbid, whether she would have to remain in the Jamaican hospital until she was stable enough to return. All of these destructive thoughts were racing through my head. I wanted to be with her, hold her, and protect her.

I could tell by Jeremy's voice that he was getting frustrated. "I have contacted the insurance company. They tell me that unless there is a hospital in our area that will accept her as a patient, they cannot send a medical plane to take her out of the country. The insurance company is requesting that Chantal's cardiologist get in touch with them and provide them with her medical history. Can you get in touch with her doctor and have her send the insurance company the information?"

"Yes, I will call her office as soon as I get off the phone."

"Louise, I promise I will do everything in my power to get Chantal out of Jamaica."

"God bless all of you for staying with Chantal, and please tell her I love her and can't wait to be near her."

"I will."

We agreed one of us would call the other as soon as we had more news.

Do you have any idea how difficult it is to get in touch with a doctor on a weekend? I called her cardiologist, and the answering service came on. I explained the situation and told her I needed to talk to the doctor. She said to me, "The doctor is not on call. Phone her office Monday morning." I could not believe it! How could this person be so insensitive? "Monday, are you kidding me? My daughter needs help now." I hung up the phone and immediately dialed Chantal's regular doctor. The service told me they would have her call as soon as they could reach her. I had no idea when that would be. I cried as I sat and waited. All I could do now was put my trust in God and Jeremy, who to this day I call My Living Angel.

Waiting for the call gave me time to think straight. I knew getting all upset would only cause me more grief. I couldn't tie up the phone to call Alain at work until the doctor called me back. Once I received the call, I would know what to do. While I was waiting for the doctor to call, I had no idea what was happening in Jamaica.

Months prior to this, my husband and I had begun to make some positive changes in our lives. We started to read self-help books and listen to meditation tapes. We also discovered a self-healing technique that would help us to relax and reduce stress. It is a simple process where you use hand positions that activate one or more of four centers located on the head and neck. You say a prayer and set your intention, which in my case at that moment was to rid myself of this fear that was overtaking my entire body. I decided this was the perfect time to practice. I sat down in the living room, took a deep breath, and started to work on my fear. I did the process on myself. It brought me to a state of peace and calmness. This technique can also be done on another person or sent long-distance if the person is not present. Since I was so scared for my daughter, I decided to send her some healing energy.

There are many forms of energy healing techniques available. None of these are to be used as a substitute for medical or professional care. Most of them are a means for relaxation and relieving stress. Healing can appear in many forms. There can be a physical healing, an emotional healing, and a spiritual healing. For me at that time the technique was an emotional healing.

Soon after, the phone rang. It was Jeremy. "I finally spoke to the doctor again, I mentioned to him that after a stroke a patient needs to take an antithrombolytic pill to lessen the side effects of the stroke. The doctor told me that if I didn't care for the way he was treating Chantal to take her elsewhere. Unfortunately, that is exactly what we had to do, move her to another hospital. The care at this hospital is an improvement, but the conditions are no better." The situation there seemed to be getting worse instead of better. I felt so helpless. "The doctor has given Chantal some medication to make her feel better. She is resting comfortably right now." I was very happy to hear those words.

"The doctor has not called back yet."

"That's okay. I was talking to the insurance company. They tell me they no longer need Chantal's medical records. I have contacted my boss at the hospital where I work. He told me even if he had to put a bed in the hallway, he would make sure Chantal is brought home." Jeremy worked at a small-town hospital with limited beds. Having a bed available for Chantal in this hospital would permit the insurance company's authorization to move her out of Jamaica.

"Thank God for your boss. I am so grateful to him and to you." I felt a little more optimistic that God was going to make it all better. I thanked Jeremy and told him we would stay in touch.

The doctor called back as soon as I got off the phone with Jeremy. I told her the situation. She told me if there was anything she could do to let her know. I thanked her for being understanding. I tried to get a hold of Alain at work, but by this time he was on his way home. I then called Chantal's dad and her brother and explained the situation. They were very concerned and afraid for Chantal. I told them that no matter what time it was, I would call them back as soon as I received more news. It was now four o'clock. Alain finally walked in the door. I gave him a few minutes to remove his coat and boots. He saw the expression on my face and asked me what was wrong. I told him the frightening news. We both started to cry. Alain took me in his arms to comfort me. "It's going to be all right; we are going to get through this." He always seemed to know what to say to make me feel better.

Alain and I waited intently for Jeremy's next call. We had not heard anything since three, and I was getting worried. Around ten, the phone rang. Alain and I both jumped out of our chairs. It was Jeremy. I was hoping he was going to tell us Chantal was on her way home.

"Chantal is okay, resting comfortably. She is happy we are here with her. I'm still working on getting her home."

"I know you are doing everything you can. We all appreciate your helping her. Please tell her we love her. Let me know as soon as you hear something no matter what time it is."

"I will." I told Alain what Jeremy said. We were both disappointed, but we believed Jeremy was doing everything in his power to bring her home. Immediately we contacted John and Thomas, who were anxious for news.

After talking to Jeremy, I really felt the need to pray. God has always been there for me and my family. God was there for us when Chantal had cancer. God was there for us when Chantal was diagnosed with heart disease fifteen years ago. Now I trusted God was going to help us get through this ordeal and bring Chantal home safe. It was the longest night of our lives. I did not get much sleep. All I could think about was my daughter having to spend the night in that hospital. I couldn't begin to picture what she was going through. All I could do was keep praying.

Finally, Sunday morning, the phone rang. It was Jeremy. "I have wonderful news. The hospital where I work will admit Chantal. The insurance company will finally send a medical plane to get us out of the country. There will be an attending nurse and doctor on the plane. I have also received permission to accompany Chantal."

"Oh, thank God. I didn't want her to be alone with strangers."

"Chantal is stable and very excited to be going home. But unfortunately, it won't be until later tonight." The medical plane had to land in London, Ontario. From there Chantal would be taken by ambulance to the hospital near Port Elgin, less than two hours away. Jeremy figured they would probably be arriving around 10:30 that night. He told us to be waiting in the parking lot around that time.

Alain and I began to cry tears of gratitude and joy. We were so grateful and relieved that she was coming home at last. "Thank you so much, Jeremy. you are a living angel. I don't know what you look like, but when I see you I will know and give you the biggest hug and kiss."

"I would do anything for Chantal."

Alain and I then gave thanks to God. We knew God provided the help and the right people to make this miracle possible. Finally, our beautiful daughter was coming home to her family, where she belonged. I called John and Thomas and told them we were heading to Port Elgin to meet the ambulance. Thomas told us to keep him informed, and John told us he would meet us at the hospital.

The hospital near Port Elgin was three and a half hours away, but we did not care. We would have driven anywhere to be with Chantal. Later that day it began to snow. Because of the weather and the distance, we left right after supper, ensuring we would have time to get there before the ambulance arrived.

The snow was coming down heavily. It was quiet in the car. I was very nervous and felt the same for Alain. I did not speak, lest it distract him from the snow-covered road. We drove through small towns and long stretches of country roads, where the homes were far apart. The snow was relentless. There were times when we thought we were lost, as the road signs were covered in snow. Alain stopped to clean the street signs to see where we were. It was a nightmare, and I couldn't wake up.

All I could say was, "Dear God, help us get through this. If I could only see the sign for Port Elgin, I would be so grateful." Then, there it was at the next corner: the most beautiful, big green sign, "Port Elgin 3 km"! I sighed with relief and thanked God. Now Alain and I finally spoke. We made it to the hospital parking lot precisely at ten o'clock and waited for the ambulance to appear.

We were so glad to have arrived safe and sound, anxious to see and hold our beautiful daughter. We waited in the cold night for her arrival. The minutes passed. It was close to eleven, and the ambulance had not yet appeared. Then Alain's cell phone rang. It was Jeremy. "Hi, Louise. We have just arrived in London. It's snowing pretty heavy over here. There's no way Chantal is able to make the journey by ambulance. I'm trying to convince the hospital to admit her."

While Jeremy and I were on the phone, he was also communicating with the hospital. I waited as he spoke to them. Again my heart was racing. I could hear shouting back and forth as Jeremy was trying to convince the hospital the importance of allowing Chantal to be admitted there. I prayed the hospital would keep her. After waiting several minutes with great anticipation, I heard, "Louise, the hospital has agreed to admit Chantal."

Thank God, what a relief. "Jeremy I can't thank you enough for helping Chantal. I can't wait to meet you tomorrow."

"You are welcome. I am just so relieved Chantal is home."

We breathed another sigh of relief, for tonight our daughter was safe. Alain and I held each other and cried. We were so grateful to have Chantal back home, where she would receive the care she needed. Leaving the hospital lot, we went to town to find a room for the night. When we got there, Chantal's dad was reserving a room in the same hotel. What were the odds of that happening? We gave John the update and told him we would meet him for breakfast. He too was disappointed he could not see Chantal that night, but he knew it was for the best. We said good-bye and went to our rooms. We knew tomorrow was going to be a long day.

That night Alain and I lay in bed, consoling each other and trusting that everything would work out. Now was the time to put into practice what we had begun to learn, think positively, and trust that God would take care of Chantal. For me it was getting into a quiet state a form of meditation and visualization. I asked God to remove my fears and worries. I refused to allow my ego to bring negative thoughts into my head. I kept repeating positive thoughts, visualizing and affirming that Chantal was going to recover from this stroke. I trusted and believed in the process.

We rose early the next morning to a beautiful, clear, brisk day. After breakfast Alain and John looked over the route we needed to take, and off we went. It had stopped snowing overnight, and the roads were already plowed. I couldn't wait to get there.

While in the car, I was reading *The Secret*. For those of you who are not familiar with this book, *The Secret* talks about people being magnets. What we think we attract. If we think negative thoughts, we attract negativity in our lives. If we think positive, that is what we attract. This is only a brief summary; there is more to it. This is just to help you understand what I was doing. Instead of me seeing my daughter in bed sick and suffering the result of her stroke, I visualized my daughter sitting up in her bed laughing and talking with her best friend, Alissa, who was by her bedside. I kept repeating, "I am so grateful that Chantal has recovered from her stroke and that she is back to her usual healthy self." I could actually hear that special laugh of hers.

It was such an experience. I thought I was making this up, but I could actually hear her sweet voice. I became very emotional and started to cry. It was as though I was seeing the future. I did not know if it was real or if it was the emotions that made me cry. I simply allowed those feelings and emotions to happen. I trusted that this was God's way of helping me not only be positive, but to have confidence in him, the outcome, and the process.

Finally, we arrived at the London hospital. We already knew that the only bed they had available for Chantal was in the emergency ward. So we went there first. As we entered the hospital and headed towards the ER, we stopped to ask the nurse which bed she was in. She did not even have to answer. I heard my daughter's voice and her laughter.

We pulled the curtain and there she was, talking to Alissa and her mom. Her skin was bronzed from the sun; she was alive and beautiful as ever. She was exactly as I had pictured her, sitting up in her bed talking and laughing. Once again God had answered my prayers. I immediately thanked God for this blessed moment. I had been longing to hold Chantal for so long. I leaned over and held her in my arms. I couldn't stop kissing her. "Chantal I'm so glad you're home."

"Mom, I'm so happy to see all of you."

"Where is Jeremy? I can't wait to meet him." Alissa replied he had gone to get some sleep at her house and would be back later. I was a little disappointed, but I understood he needed his rest. It was Monday morning, and he had not slept since Friday night. I still had my arms around Chantal; I did not want to let her go. I knew I had to give Alain and John their turns. Alissa and her mom left the room so we could spend some family time with her. Being in the emergency ward, we were not allowed to stay very long.

We did not want to burden Chantal by having to go over all of the events she experienced. We figured Jeremy would fill us in on all the details. However, I did notice that she could not move her right arm without the help of her left arm. I was concerned but felt I should not mention it at this time.

We tried to lift Chantal's spirits by focusing on the fact that she was home safe with her family. When Chantal had to get up and go to the washroom, I asked her if she needed help. She said no, she wanted to do it by herself. I was deeply grateful that she could get up and walk on her own. As she was walking towards the bathroom, I saw that she dragged her right foot and held on to her right arm. How proud I was to see her trying to do this all on her own. This just reaffirmed the courage my beautiful daughter possessed. She never complained. This may be a little hard to understand, and I can't explain it, but it was as though she knew she needed to experience what had just happened to her. It was as though she knew this was another part of her journey. We waited for her to return, told her we had to leave and let her rest. We would be back soon. We knew how important rest was for her at this time.

We were out in the entrance area talking with Alissa and her mom, wondering when Jeremy was going to arrive. I could not wait to meet this wonderful angel. Every time a younger person would walk through the doors to the emergency room, I looked to see if it was Jeremy. I truly felt that I would know who he was.

Finally the door opened. In walked a big, tall, husky young man, his face bronzed from the sun. He reminded me of a big teddy bear. I knew it was Jeremy. I got up went directly to him and asked if he was, and he said yes. I told him we were Chantal's parents and gave him the big hug I had promised him on the phone. Since Chantal was resting, we all sat down in the waiting area and got to know each other. Jeremy went over the events leading up to that moment. By the look on his face and the sound of his voice, you could feel the compassion he had for our daughter.

He told us of his fears of maybe not being able to get her out of Jamaica, the upsetting calls to the insurance company, how the hospital was so primitive it did not have Chantal's medication on hand. Jeremy had to take a cab to a scary part of town to have a prescription filled. One of the friends had to go back to the hotel and get Chantal a blanket and pillow. He then told us that when it was time to leave the hospital, Chantal gave her blanket and pillow to a patient in need. Jeremy explained how the three of them decided not to fly out that night and chose to be with Chantal regardless of the extra expenses. All they cared about was Chantal and getting her home safe.

This is what I call true friends: people who are unselfish and will put others who are in need ahead of themselves, people who will remain with you till the end, no matter what. God bless each and every one of you for staying with our daughter.

In the meantime, Chantal had woken up, and we were able to go back for a short visit. We sent Jeremy in first; as we felt she would want to see him after all they had endured together. We then took brief turns going in. I could see by Chantal's face this whole ordeal had taking a toll on her. I believe she finally realized what actually happened to her. Chantal was weak and very tired. She couldn't keep her eyes open; she told us she wanted to sleep. It was getting late, so we told Chantal we would be back first thing in the morning, as we kissed her good-bye. We were all exhausted after such a long day, both physically and emotionally. I thanked God for taking care of my baby and for returning her safely back home to us.

The next day Chantal was still in the ER, because there were no beds available on the wards. But my daughter was feeling much better now that she was back home and being cared for. She had her beautiful big smile on as we entered her room. She was glad to see us once again. Chantal told us the hospital was looking to move her to another floor that day. She was still having some difficulty with her right arm, but her walk had improved slightly. Even the nurse came in and told us Chantal was doing great. Alain and I had taken the week off work; however, John had to go back. He felt comfortable leaving Chantal. He could see she was on the road to recovery. Besides, he wanted to go back home and give Thomas the news.

Her dear friend Alissa was also a big part of the healing process. She was another angel. When Alissa was not working, she spent a lot of her time with Chantal during recovery. She always made sure Chantal was kept comfortable. She brought her magazine and treats and played cards with her. I was grateful to Alissa, because most of the time she would come and visit Chantal after supper. This gave Alain and me the opportunity to go back to Chantal's apartment to relax and keep her cat Spencer company. By Wednesday they finally had a bed for Chantal, and she could leave the emergency ward. I was very grateful to the ER staff for taking good care of our daughter.

Chantal was feeling better; she was starting to eat solid foods. She was slowly regaining some of her strength too, but therapy was urgently needed for her right leg and arm. By Friday, Chantal was transferred to Parkwood, a hospital that specialized in stroke patients. Chantal understood the need to go to this hospital. The quicker she healed, the sooner she could go back to work. This was her goal: to get back to her job as soon as possible. Once we arrived at the hospital, we helped Chantal settle in.

The nurse came in and took Chantal's vitals. She told us a cardiologist would be coming to talk to us. When he came in, he introduced himself, and Chantal proceeded to give him an account of what had happened to her. He then examined her.

He said, "From what I can see Chantal you will need to do physiotherapy and occupational therapy to get your strength and mobility back in your leg and your arm. After you have completed the exercises we will then see if there is any further therapy needed. Once you are discharged from the hospital, you will have to be off work for at least six weeks. Having a stroke can cause not only physical but emotional damage. If you find yourself getting depressed, let me know. I can give you medication for it."

"I will, doctor." He shook our hands, said good-bye, and left.

After the conversation with the doctor, Chantal had a look of despair on her face. She looked as if she were going to cry. I looked at her and said, "Chantal you are going to get through this. You will be back to work before you know it."

"I don't want to be here. I want to go home."

"I know, honey, but it can't be helped." I believe that after all that happened to Chantal, it finally started to sink in that she might have a long road ahead of her. I could see that she was upset.

Chantal wanted out of there and back to work *now*. I encouraged her to be patient and promised to do the self-healing technique on her to help speed up her recovery. It was vital to keep her spirits up, especially at this time in her life. The look on her face was heartbreaking. As a mother, when you see your child sad, hurting, or even afraid, you want to take away all the pain and anguish they are going through. Unfortunately, there are times when it is out of our control, and there is nothing else we can do but love them, support them, and pray to God to look after them.

It was the weekend, so it was pretty quiet in the hospital. We stayed with Chantal most of the day, and in the evening Alissa came to keep her company. Alain had to go back to work. He left on Sunday after supper. I was alone with Chantal's cat Spencer in the apartment. I couldn't even imagine what Chantal was going through or what she had experienced in Jamaica. She had shown such strength up until now. I wanted to take away all her pain, but I knew I couldn't. She would be the one having to go through this. After crying for a while, I decided it was time to stop feeling sorry for myself and do a meditation and send healing to my daughter.

By Monday morning, the doctor had Chantal start physiotherapy. Chantal's leg had improved considerably on its own, but she still had difficulty with her arm. With perseverance and determination, Chantal completed all the exercises necessary for recovery by the end of the week. She now had full use of her right leg and was able to raise her right arm without any assistance. Chantal was determined to do everything they asked of her to get better. Her goal was to go home and back to work as soon as possible. I believe the healings I performed on her twice a day certainly helped in achieving this goal.

The doctor was so pleased with Chantal's recovery that he allowed her to go home on a weekend pass. What a treat for Chantal. She was excited to be in her own place and spend time with Spencer. Her friends came to stay with her, giving me the opportunity to return to my home, sleep in my own bed, and get some blessed rest.

Chantal was now going on her second week at the hospital, and I was still doing healings on her twice a day. I remember one day the doctor came in and after examining Chantal he said to her, "I can't believe how much you have improved; you look wonderful. Whatever you are doing, keep it up. I would love to send you home today; unfortunately, you have to remain here until your exercise program is completed. You might be able to go home by the end of this week." Chantal and I looked at each other, and she had a smile a mile wide. She and I both knew the healings I was performing on her had a lot to do with her speedy recovery.

Her next step was to work with the occupational therapist. It was very important that they give her exercises to regain the strength in her right arm. The therapist had her do an exercise where she would put differently shaped pegs into certain holes. In the beginning, Chantal had difficulty doing this. She would get frustrated and annoyed with herself, because it was such a simple task and yet she was having such trouble. On the first day, Chantal got very emotional. She said to me, "I now understand what my patients feel and what they go through when they can't do a certain thing." I reminded her she was fortunate that she would get better by doing these exercises. For some of them, that would never be the case.

The hospital had Chantal swimming twice a week and working on various exercise machines. They even had a five-pin bowling alley, in which, I am embarrassed to say, my daughter beat me. I told her I was going to tell everyone that my daughter who had a stroke a few weeks ago just beat me at bowling. She started to laugh. I was glad she beat me. It gave her more confidence and faith that she was going to get through all of this and be back to her usual self.

Also, the wonderful support and visits from all her family and friends certainly helped with her recovery. By the end of the week, Chantal was able to put all the little pegs in their proper place. She was now able to raise her right arm without any help. Her right leg was back to normal. The only thing that was not quite perfect was her handwriting. Her letters remained very small and close together for some time.

At the end of her second week at Parkwood, Chantal had completed all the necessary exercises, and the doctor had signed her discharge papers. She could go home. Alain had come down from St. Catharines to pick me up, and it was time for us to leave. She had one of her friends coming to stay for the weekend, so she would not be alone. Although Chantal wanted and needed me, it was important that she spend time away from her parents, and I understood that.

Never take it personally when your child does not want you around. It has nothing to do with you. Everyone sometimes needs to be alone or with friends, rather than a parent.

Chantal was still not able to stay on her own for the next six weeks. She could not drive, and she had many doctor appointments. So she did need me for this. My work was accommodating, and I was able to care for her during that time. While I was staying with her, I continued to do healings on her twice a day. After a month, she started doing the healings on herself; this way she would know how to do them during my absence. In the beginning, at the hospital, we had talked about me doing this technique on her, and Chantal had agreed. When she saw how quickly she was improving, she started to believe she was going to get better. She continued to do the healings for a long time. Day by day, Chantal was improving. She would help with the cleaning, the laundry, even the cooking. We would go shopping together and go to her doctor's appointments, but best of all was going out for lunch. This was something we both loved to do.

Chantal had many friends come to visit, so this gave me the opportunity to go back home every weekend to be with Alain and Oliver, my cat. We needed time away from each other. Because of what she was going through, being around me every minute of every day could sometimes get tense. We could easily get on each other's nerves. I remember one occasion where we exchanged words. Chantal was always good at taking her medication on time. However, that day, for some reason, she forgot to take her heart pill. Being a mother and concerned, I got all upset. I started shouting, "How can you forget to take your pills? Do you not realize how important it is to take your

medicine on time? You need to take better care of your health."
The words just came out; I couldn't stop myself.

Chantal was crying. "I do know, it's the first time I forgot, okay? Get off my case. Why don't you go home? I can take care of myself." She ran to her room and slammed the door.

I sat down and took a deep breath. "Oh my God. What did I just do?" I couldn't believe I had reacted this way. Chantal did not need this. I felt so bad. I waited a few minutes to give us both time to cool off. Then I went to her room and told her I was going for a short ride. I needed to get away. I had to leave and give her some space. I went to the grocery store and picked up a few things for supper that night. I wasn't gone long. When I came back, Chantal was in the living room watching television. I put the bags down on the counter walked towards her. She stood up, and we both hugged each other.

"Honey, I am so sorry I yelled at you. Please forgive me? I've been so worried about you."

"I know, Mom I'm sorry too. I didn't mean what I said. I know you're here to help me."

It was a very intense moment for both of us. We felt so much better after.

There are events and circumstances in our lives that are not always pleasant, especially when it comes to our health. I am a true believer that you can find something positive in every difficult situation. There are also many lessons that you can learn from a crisis. Being around my daughter for all those weeks brought us even closer than we had ever been before.

During this time of struggle, I learned to become more patient, more understanding, and more compassionate towards her. For that I am truly grateful.

In April 2008, nine weeks after her stroke, Chantal was able to return to work. That was the best news for her. After all these weeks, going back to her job meant so much to her. Finally, her life was going to go back to some degree of normality. In my heart, I believe that her determination, her constant focus on getting back to her job, and the daily healings helped her recover more quickly.

Chapter 6

Finding Love

As it was time for Chantal to begin the next phase of her life after suffering this stroke, I now needed to go home to my daily routine. It was difficult to leave her side after what we went through, but I knew this part of our journey together needed to end. It was Friday, and Alain was coming to pick me up after work. Chantal had invited a friend over for the weekend. We decided to cook a nice meal and all of us have supper together. We finished dessert, and it was time to say our good-byes. I held Chantal in my arms. Tears were running down my face, and with a hoarse voice I said, "Chantal, I love you so much, and I am so proud of you. I will miss our time together. Take good care of yourself."

"I will call you often. I love you, Mom. Thanks for everything you did for me. I really appreciate it. Don't worry; I will be fine. I will remember to take my medicine."

We both laughed. Alain took her in his arms and gave her a big hug. "I love you too, Chantal. If you need anything, don't be afraid to call us."

"I will."

It was a sad moment for all of us that evening. I gave her one last hug and kiss. Pulling out of that driveway brought more tears to my eyes. Alain held me. "Louise, everything is going to be fine." I admit, at first I worried about her health and living alone, but eventually it became easier. Chantal was a strong woman, with guts and determination. With all the love and support she received from family and friends, she would be okay. We talked on the phone often, and a few weeks later, Chantal told me that she and one of her girlfriends were moving in together. I was so pleased. It was such a relief to know that she would have someone to keep her company, as well as share the rent. For the next two years Chantal went on to improve.

In July of 2009 my husband surprised me with a cruise to Alaska. It was a week-long cruise chartered by Louise Hay of Hay House Publishing. Louise's books have helped thousands of people all over the world. Her *You Can Heal Your Life* was one of the first books that helped change my life. The "I Can Do It" conferences are held every year in different parts of the world. That year it was called "I Can Do It at Sea." There were many famous authors on the ship. I had signed up to do four-day workshops with world-renowned psychic Sylvia Browne and famous medium Colette Baron Reid. I had first seen Sylvia on television and had read many of her books; meeting her was a dream come true.

Attending these workshops changed my life forever. It was such a great experience. When Sylvia told the audience we were all born with psychic abilities, I was amazed. I thought only special people were born with this wonderful gift. I vowed to myself that upon my return I was going to pursue this.

Since the trip I had been asking my angels and guides to help me get in touch with someone to help me on my spiritual journey. It was a Monday morning about nine months later when I was leaving the local health food store that I heard a voice whisper, "Spirituality." I immediately stopped, then turned to my left. On the wall was a bulletin board covered with business cards, along with this pink eight-by-ten flyer offering a meditation and spiritual development class. Finally, this was the answer to my prayer. It was exactly what I had been searching for. I took down the information and called as soon as I got home.

My appointment to see Reverend Anita was set for Friday. I couldn't wait to meet her. Finally, the day arrived. Anita opened the door, and the first thing I noticed was her radiant smile and friendly personality. Anita is a petite woman, standing five feet four inches tall, and has shoulder-length blonde hair. I immediately felt a wonderful energy around her. She introduced herself and invited me in. She directed me to her office, and we began to talk.

Anita was not only a medium; she could also do hands-on healing. I agreed to have a healing done on me. The warmth radiating from her hands as she laid them on my shoulders, my knees, and my back was something I had never experienced. This brought tears to my eyes. The healing took about forty minutes, and throughout that time I felt such peace within.

We then sat and talked for almost two hours. I told her that becoming a medium and healer was a lifelong dream. Her classes would help me achieve my goal and start me on my spiritual journey. I immediately signed up. That day Anita also gave me literature on the Fellowships of the Spirit, where she received her ministerial ordination. It is a wonderful school in Lily Dale, New York, located just outside the gates of a spiritual community established in 1879. The school is run by co-founder and director Reverend Elaine Thomas.

I thanked Anita and told her I would see her in class the following Saturday. When I got home, I read the book from front to back. It listed all the different workshops and trainings available. The book mentioned how the school was able to teach you how to enhance your intuitive gifts and also perform various healing techniques. I signed up for the first training in May and the second in September, and in November 2010 I signed up for the two-year program. It did not take long for me to feel the presence of spirit and receive wonderful healing messages to give to my classmates. With the help of the wonderful teachers and the school, I was able to learn to enhance my natural psychic-mediumistic skills and learn different healing techniques. I am so grateful to God for opening up these doors, for my friend Anita, and the school for helping me on my spiritual path.

June 2012, with hard work and determination, I graduated, receiving my ministerial ordination. What a proud day that was for my family and me. By October I had set up my own website. I have a room in my home I call my sacred space, where I meditate, offer healings, and bring messages from spirit, guides, and angels to my clients. I believe God opened up these doors for me, and I took full advantage of these wonderful opportunities. I am so grateful I am who I am today.

In November 2010 Chantal turned twenty-seven. She was able to work enough to buy a small townhouse. Good things started to happen for Chantal, and God knows she deserved it. Having her own place was a big step, and it gave her pleasure to be able to decorate it the way she wanted.

A few months after she moved into her townhouse, Chantal and Thomas had talked about him moving in with her. Because of his work, two years prior Thomas had moved to Hamilton, about forty minutes from St. Catharines. Due to cutbacks he lost his job. He decided to take a year-long course for his trade. It was closer to get to school from London, where Chantal lived, than from Hamilton. They both agreed that moving in together would help her with household expenses, and they could also get to know each other better as adults. Because of the twelve-year age difference, they did not hang out together as brother and sister. This move would provide them that opportunity.

Chantal was a real social butterfly. If Chantal was not at work, she would be out with friends. When the sister of one of her many friends decided to get married in the Dominican Republic, Chantal was invited. When I found out I was not pleased. I was still trying to be positive after everything that already happened in her life, but when she told me this, I flashed back to her trip to Jamaica. I knew nothing I was going to say to her was going to stop her from going. When Chantal had her heart set on something, nothing and no one was going to stop her. The only thing I could do was pray to God to protect her, keep her safe, and send her healing energy. I told her to call me as soon as she got back home. She agreed she would call me on her cell phone as soon as the plane landed. That was all I could ask for. In the end, everything turned out to be wonderful, and she had the time of her life. What a relief that was for me!

Chantal enjoyed being around her friends. She had dated occasionally, but now she was feeling the need to have someone special in her life. Being the person she was, she felt that if she met someone she liked, it was important for her to let them know of her health problems. Not every man would want to take on this responsibility. I told her that I felt it was not necessary to tell everyone that she dated, only the one who was interested in continuing the relationship. Chantal told me she would know when it would be the right time.

Eventually she met Adam, and she had someone in her life at last. She called me up one day to tell me. She was so excited on the phone. "Mom, I've met someone. His name is Adam. We've been dating for a little while."

"That's wonderful! What's he look like?"

"He is good-looking, tall, slim, and has dark hair. Mom, we went out a few times, and I felt right telling him about my health problems, and he still wants to see me."

"Oh, dear, I am so happy for you."

"Adam has even come to some of my doctor's appointments with me."

"That's great. I don't know too many guys that would do that."

"Me neither. Mom, I can talk to him and he listens. He even told me how beautiful I was."

"You are, dear."

"He's coming over for supper tonight."

"I'm really happy for you I'm glad you have someone in your life you deserve it."

"Thanks, Mom. I have to go get ready."

"I love you, dear."

"I love you, Mom." Chantal never had a problem telling anyone she cared for how much she loved them. It always came natural to her.

Chantal and Adam started spending more time together. They had been dating for approximately six months, when, around May, Adam moved in with Chantal. My son was finished school and now looking for employment. Thomas thought there would be more opportunity for work in the London area, but it turned out he found a job here in St. Catharines. It was a perfect time for Adam to move in. Chantal would call me up and tell me how the two of them were able to talk about everything and how he kept telling her how beautiful she was. My daughter was beautiful outside, but I feel Adam could see her inner beauty as well.

By the end of this blissful summer, Chantal was starting to notice some changes in her health. She was retaining water and having more problems with breathing. Chantal's lungs filled with fluids a few times. They had to put her on antibiotics and increase her fluid pills. Her lungs would clear up for a while, and they would start to fill up again. There were nights when she would sleep propped up. Chantal never wanted to worry us, and many times she kept this from me. She always thought of others before herself. I can't imagine how frightening it must have been for her. The doctor changed her water pills and increased the dosage, but it never lasted long enough for her to have some comfort. This went on for over a year.

Because of her health problems, she was missing more work, and this was causing more strain. Chantal told the doctor that something had to be done. She could not continue to live this way. Her cardiologist finally sent her to another heart specialist, and they both agreed that Chantal needed to have her bicuspid valve repaired or replaced with a mechanical one. Thank God her best friend, Alissa, was with her when she received the news.

Chantal was scheduled for admission to the London hospital for major surgery on Friday, March 23, 2012. For the last seventeen years, with the aid of medication the leaking of the valve was under control. After Chantal's stroke the valve opening was stretched even more. This allowed the excess blood to go backwards into the heart, causing her shortness of breath and fatigue. They would either repair or replace the valve. The week before her surgery, my husband and I, Chantal, Adam, and Alissa needed to go to the hospital for a three-hour consultation. It was crucial for us to know what to do or expect after the operation and during Chantal's recovery. We would have to watch a video of the surgery itself, then speak with a psychologist, nutritionist, social worker, and a head nurse from the ICU.

Alain and I drove to London and picked up Chantal, Adam, and Alissa. A nurse directed us to a room where she set up the video and informed us someone would be in shortly to talk to us. Seeing the patient on the tape lying there with all these tubes in him was scary to me. I had to ask Chantal how she felt watching this. She replied, "If this is what I need to go through to have a better quality of life, I will do whatever it takes. I can't stand not be able to breathe properly and looking like I'm six months pregnant." Because of the fluid retention, Chantal's stomach was always big. That really bothered her.

The first person to come in the room was a nutritionist. She explained to Chantal how crucial it was for her to watch her sodium intake. She gave her a list of foods she could eat and those she needed to stay away from. Because Chantal loved to eat, she found some of these restrictions most difficult.

The next person was the nurse working in ICU. She explained her role in caring for Chantal after the surgery: changing and removing the tubes, administering the medication, and making sure Chantal was kept comfortable. She explained that any surgery had possible risks, such as bleeding or high or low blood pressure. They would give her medication to stabilize the problem. In any case, Chantal needed to be aware of any possibilities.

The next doctor was the psychologist. It was important for her to see what state of mind Chantal was in. She wanted to know if Chantal was mentally and emotionally ready to have the surgery. Did she understand why the surgery was needed? Did she understand the risks involved? Besides family support, did Chantal have outside support?

The last person to see was the social worker. She explained the financial support that was available to Chantal during her time off work. This was important information, as Chantal had no sick benefits at her job, so she had to rely on disability unemployment benefits. The woman talked about different means of transportation to and from the hospital. She also gave us a list of places and contact numbers we might need. A lot of this information would be of great use. After the consultation we took Chantal out to one of her favourite restaurants. Upon our return home I called John, Thomas, and the rest of the family to give them the update. I heard the voices of concern on the other end. Everyone assured me they would send prayers.

On Monday before the surgery, Chantal called me to see if she could come home for a few days. Of course we welcomed her. It would give us another opportunity to see each other and have a good talk. She told me she would be arriving the next day. I couldn't wait to see her.

Tuesday afternoon I received a call from Chantal. "Hi, Mom. I'm in St. Catharines. I'm over at Cathy's. She invited me for supper. I won't be home too late. See you when I get there."

"That's okay, dear. I'll see you later." Chantal went straight to her friend Cathy's. This was definitely okay with me. They had supper together and shared what they would have never thought to be the last time they ever saw each other.

Her week at camp as a companion, eighteen years old

Enjoying another week at camp

Bridesmaid at my wedding, eighteen years old

At age nineteen doing what she loved best: cooking

I waited until eleven, and Chantal still wasn't home. I decided to go to bed, but I couldn't sleep until I knew she was home in her bed. All of sudden I heard the door unlock. I got up to greet her at the door and help her with her suitcase. "Hi, honey, I'm so glad to see you."

"Hi, Mom." I immediately embraced her. "Are you hungry?"

"No, I ate at Cathy's. I'm really tired. Can we talk tomorrow?"

"Sure we can."

She got ready for bed, and I decided to tuck her in as I did when she was little. "Good-night, dear. I love you."

"Good-night, Mom. I love you too."

The next morning after breakfast, Chantal and I sat in the living room and talked. "How are you feeling, Chantal? Are you afraid of what can happen?"

"Mom, I'm terrified. This is a big operation."

"I know, dear. It has to be scary." For the first time Chantal admitted to me she was frightened.

"If surgery is going to make me feel better, then I'll go through it. I can't live this way anymore. There are times I can't catch my breath and it scares me."

"Why wouldn't you tell me this?"

"I did not want to worry you."

"Why do you feel you have to go through all of this alone? I'm your mother. I want to help you."

"I'm sorry, Mom." We were both in tears.

Once again her courage and determination inspired me. She talked about Adam and how supportive he was throughout this ordeal. I was so grateful to Adam for being a part of her life. We also talked about why the soul keeps coming back to learn life's lessons, and why and how we pick this particular life. Although Chantal understood the process, she asked me why she came into this lifetime with all these different illnesses. I had an idea why. I told her I would do a past-life retrieval on her, to see if we could get an answer.

When I do a past life retrieval on a client, it gives me information on who they were in a past life and what quality traits they have carried over from that lifetime into this lifetime.

I went into my room meditated, grounded, and centered myself. I do this by taking in three deep breaths to relax and allow the white light of the Holy Spirit to come down from the centre of my head (crown chakra) all the way down through every part of my body, right down to the bottom of my feet. I then set my intention by asking God, the angels, loved ones who have crossed over, my guides, and, at that time, Chantal's guides to give me an answer to her question. Suddenly during my meditation, I felt my mother's presence. I was a little surprised to feel her beside me. I asked her what she was doing here; she never uttered a word but simply stood by my side. I experienced a peaceful feeling and knew that she was here for support. I called Chantal to come into the room and began to give her the reading.

"Chantal, I see a young boy around seven or eight years old. He tells me his name is Joshua. He is performing healings. I see a lot of people with different illnesses lined up waiting for their turn. Joshua is laying his hands on each one. Some of them are falling to the ground. They can feel Joshua's energy coming from his touch. The healing is penetrating right through their bodies. Each person Joshua has touched is healed. Those who couldn't walk are walking. Others have regained their sight, and others are healed of their disease." I couldn't believe what I was feeling or seeing; it was an incredible experience. It was as though I were watching a video of all that was happening. Chantal sat there silently. The healings were shown to me for only a few minutes. I thought, *How is this information going to help in answering Chantal's question?* At that moment I received the answer.

Every person that Joshua touched believed, trusted, and had faith that Joshua could heal them. This was a big part of the healing process. The compassion and love that this boy had for these strangers was God-sent. Joshua looked at everyone as a child of God and was grateful that he possessed the gift of healing. The reason Chantal came to earth with all her illnesses was for her to experience the pain and anguish that these strangers who came to Joshua felt.

To better understand, I will explain that every one of us comes here on earth to experience different lessons in life. We take on different lifetimes, "reincarnation," to experience these lessons. Chantal was Joshua in a past life. As Joshua, she knew she could heal, but she did not feel what they felt. So in this lifetime, Chantal chose to feel the pain of having her illnesses. For example, after her stroke, during one of Chantal's occupational therapy sessions, she had difficulty putting the small peg in the proper hole. Working with people with brain injuries, she was able to feel what they felt when they were unable to do certain tasks. As I explained this past life to her, she was able to understand why she chose this life. She also told me if she ever had a son, she wanted to call him Joshua.

It was Thursday, the day before Chantal's surgery. Alain, Chantal, and I had to return to London. Chantal had to be at the hospital for Friday morning. None of us had much sleep that night. I had prayed to God and the angels to watch over Chantal during the surgery and keep her safe. While we were waiting for Chantal to be admitted, I happened to turn towards her. She was sitting on Adam's lap. Alissa had said something funny, and Chantal started laughing. They were joking back and forth. She didn't seem scared. It was not what you would expect from someone going in for major surgery. But then again, Chantal was not just someone. She was a special soul. At that moment I felt so proud of my daughter.

We were able to stay with her until it was time for her surgery. The cardiologist who was going to perform the surgery came in and introduced himself to us. He asked Chantal how she was feeling. She told him she was scared but was ready to get this over. He explained the surgery would take about eight hours. There would be about seven doctors, including a few nurses in the room to assist him. He was going to try and repair her valve; however, if it was beyond repair, he would have to replace it with a mechanical one. She would be given medication to ease the pain and discomfort. Full recovery from this type of surgery would take at least three months. Once the operation was over, he would come and talk to us and let us know how things went during the surgery. The doctor told Chantal he felt confident this procedure would improve her quality of life. She was glad to hear him say that.

Soon after, the anesthesiologist came in and told Chantal not to worry. His job was to make sure Chantal slept through the operation. The nurse had Chantal sign the necessary papers. It was time for us to say our good-byes. I leaned over, held Chantal close to me, gave her a kiss, and whispered, "Honey, before you go to sleep, call on the archangel Raphael to be with you, and to send you healing for a quick recovery after the surgery."

"I will, Mom."

Alain, Alissa, and Adam then gave Chantal their best wishes. Chantal remained calm and tried to stay positive. I know she felt scared inside, but she never showed it. She was such a brave girl. As usual, she did not want us to worry. When they wheeled my beautiful daughter away, my heart went out to her. I was scared. I hated the fact she had to go through this ordeal. I felt such sadness weighing on my heart. If I could have taken her place on the operating table, I would have.

The orderly came and took Chantal around ten. We went and sat in the waiting room, knowing it was going to be a long day. We kept ourselves busy reading, doing jigsaw puzzles, talking, pacing the floor, and reading some more. We watched other people experiencing what we were experiencing, waiting for news about their loved ones. We did everything possible to keep our minds occupied during this frightening time. At

11:30 that morning, Alain and I went to a small chapel on the main floor, to pray for Chantal, to ask God to watch over her throughout the surgery and grant her a speedy recovery.

We continued to keep busy throughout the day. By eight o'clock that night, the time for the surgery was beyond the original eight hours. I was getting worried. I kept repeating to myself *Everything was going to be okay. Maybe they started the operation later than they had planned. The doctor did say he would come and speak with us.* I looked around the room and saw that we were now the last ones waiting. I was getting really concerned. *Maybe he forgot, or maybe something has gone wrong.* It was a long day trying to keep positive, but at this moment I really had to work hard at letting go of my negative thoughts.

Finally, around 9:30, the doctor entered the room. He looked physically exhausted. He asked us to follow him into a private area. I did not like the sound of those words. My heart started pounding really fast. For a few seconds I thought, *Oh God, what if something happened to Chantal?* I immediately dismissed that thought.

He began to explain. "The surgery took a few more hours than we had originally thought. I was hoping to repair her leaky valve, but unfortunately, it was beyond repair, and I had to put in a mechanical one. The next twenty-four hours will determine how the surgery went."

I asked, "Is Chantal going to be okay?"

"She is young, and I feel optimistic that she will have a good recovery."

"Will the mechanical one work the same way as her own?"

"Yes, it will work the same as her valve did."

"When can we see her?"

"Please wait at least another hour until the nurses clean her up. You will have to take turns going in."

"Thank you, doctor."

By eleven, we were all very anxious to see Chantal. It was as though time stood still. The hour seemed to take forever. One of the nurses finally gave us permission to go in one at a time. I immediately stood up, turned to Alain, Adam, and Alissa, and said, "Sorry, guys. I'm her mother and I'm going in first." At that moment, I could think only of me. I was going to be the face Chantal saw when she opened her eyes. They agreed.

I followed the nurse as she took me down several hallways to the intensive care unit. When the nurse pulled the curtains open, I could not believe my eyes. Looking at my daughter with all those tubes connected to her was terrifying. I had seen the video prior to her surgery but had no idea what to expect until I saw it with my own eyes. There were tubes everywhere: in her throat, on her sides, some in her chest, and in her neck. The areas were all covered in blood. It broke my heart to see my beautiful daughter that way. I just wanted to burst out crying.

She was starting to wake up, so I did not want her to see the fear on my face. That was the last thing she needed. What do you say to someone who has just come out of major surgery? "How are you feeling?" It sounds pretty silly, considering what she had just gone through.

"Hi honey, it's all over. The doctor told us he could not repair your own valve; he had to put in an artificial one." She blinked her eyes to show me she understood. "I love you so much. I'm so proud of you. I can only stay for a few minutes. Alain, Adam, and Alissa are waiting their turn. We are all here for you." She did not say much. She nodded that she understood. I could see she was also glad it was over.

Everyone had a chance to visit briefly with Chantal. It was now time for her to rest. It had been a long, trying day, and we were exhausted mentally, emotionally, and physically. It was after midnight when we left the hospital parking lot. Luckily, Chantal had an extra bedroom. Alain and I were able to stay there with Adam and Spencer. That night I sent Chantal prayers and healings. I asked God to send her strength and courage for the months to follow.

The next morning, Alain and I arrived at the hospital at nine. We didn't know that visiting hours started at eleven. We decided to spend some of that time in the hospital chapel and pray. I was hoping Chantal had gotten a good night's sleep and wasn't in any pain. This time the nurse allowed Alain and me to go in together. Chantal was still groggy with the painkillers they were giving her, but when she saw the two of us, she had a smile on her face. She couldn't talk; she just listened and nodded. We kept telling her how much we loved her and how proud we were.

Since Chantal was in ICU, it was very difficult for me to perform healings on her. The ward was always so busy, the nurses and doctors coming in and out all the time. I had to do healings from home. Every night just before I went to sleep, I would meditate and visualize my daughter in bed and send her the healing.

When I do healings either in person or long-distance, I prepare myself in the same way I prepare myself for a reading, only my intention is different. I call on Jesus and the archangels Michael and Raphael to assist me in sending energy healing to that person. For those of you who do not know about the archangels, Michael is our protector, and Raphael is our healer. With the client in front of me, I stand with my hands on his or her shoulders, where I ground and centre myself. My hands then feel guided to areas on the body that need the healing. I ask that the person receive this healing for his or her highest good. In my daughter's case, I visualized the white light going through her entire body as she lay there.

Three days after the surgery, the doctor removed Chantal's breathing tube. That was one of the tubes Chantal dreaded the most. Having this inside her throat was uncomfortable, and she was unable to speak. She was relieved when it came out. Every day for the first week she was showing small signs of improvement. We kept taking turns going in to see her. The doctors had cut back on some of the drugs for pain. She was breathing more easily, and her morale was positive. Since the worst was over and Chantal was getting better, my husband and Adam felt they could go back to work. I stayed for as long as Chantal needed me.

The following week in ICU, Chantal continued to improve. The doctor had removed a few more tubes. She was slowly introduced to liquids. She no longer needed her pain medication, but she still needed a lot of rest to build her strength. Unfortunately, Chantal's bed was directly beside the nurse's station. She could hear the nurses talking, and that kept her awake. I stayed with Chantal throughout the days. Sometimes we just sat there quietly. Other times we read or talked about her cat, Spencer, or what we were going to do when she came home. When she got tired I would leave and let her rest.

Adam would come every afternoon after work and keep us company. It was great having him around. I would see her eyes light up when she saw him coming around the corner. I would leave the room to give them time together. I did not know this, but her friend Alissa would come later and stay with Chantal until ten or eleven at night. When Alissa told me this, I was so glad. Some nights when I kissed Chantal good-bye, I felt guilty leaving her. Having her friend there to keep her company was a relief for me. Even one of the nurses told me she was happy to have Alissa there. It made her work easier. She pampered Chantal and took the time to read, talk to her, and keep her company. Chantal always looked up to her. Alissa knew exactly what to say to make her feel better.

By the third week, the only tube remaining was the one on the side of her neck. I continued to do healings on Chantal to speed up her recovery. A few days later the nurse came in and told Chantal she was going to remove the last tube. It was a day for celebration. Chantal was ecstatic. "Finally, I can move around." She took a deep breath, something she was not able to do for a long time. "God, it feels good to be able to breathe again." She was so grateful that her breathing had improved. She was free at last. She could walk, sit up, wash herself, and eat solid food. What a victory!

Chantal's appetite was not the greatest, especially because it was hospital food. Due to sodium restrictions, the food was very bland, and she would not eat it. The doctors and the nurses were concerned that Chantal was not consuming enough calories to regain her strength. They put her on high-protein shakes, which were not to her liking.

I too was concerned about her eating. She was not gaining weight, and after a major surgery she needed to build her strength to heal faster. To get her to eat, I was willing to pick up any foods that she wanted. One day she asked me for an Arby's, and I brought it in. When the head nurse saw the bag, she pulled me aside and gave me royal heck. She told me that this was the worst thing she could eat, that it was loaded with sodium. I never even thought of it. All I could focus on was getting her to eat. It was upsetting to both of us. The nurse did apologize later. I understood she too was concerned for Chantal's well-being.

Chantal really did try to drink her protein shakes. It took her hours to finish them. Watching her slowly drinking those shakes reminded me of when she was a little girl. She would be going in for a scan and had to drink yet another awful drink. I would play a game with her, where she would take one big sip, and I would show her the level she was at on the glass. Then I would encourage her to take another sip and then another one, and before we knew it, the drink was all gone. I did this with her when she was four years old, and now I was playing the game with her at the age of twenty-nine. I must say it did not work as well this time.

At the end of the fourth week, Chantal was released from the hospital. Finally, I could take her home. It was the end of April. It was a beautiful, sunny Friday afternoon. Chantal had texted Adam at work to meet us at home. She could not wait to see Spencer, either. It was a twenty-minute drive from the hospital to Chantal's place. All she talked about in the car was being with Adam, sleeping in her own bed, and holding Spencer. She missed him so much.

During the time Chantal spent in the hospital, Spencer felt lost. He would roam from room to room looking for her. He too really missed her. When Chantal came through the front door, Spencer immediately went to her. Animals can sense when things are different. They have feelings, just as we humans do, and Spencer knew there was something going on with his mistress. Now he would not leave her sight for very long.

I had been staying in London for over a month. Now, with Chantal being home with Adam and Spencer to keep her company, I was able to have a break and go home for the weekend. I was a little nervous leaving her, but I felt she was in good hands. I would return Sunday night to care for Chantal during the week. I missed my husband and my own cat, Oliver. Alain had come to visit Chantal in the hospital a few times, but being home again for a few days would be treasured. When I opened the door, Alain was there to greet me with open arms. We hugged and kissed. I felt such comfort, such relief, as if a ton of bricks was lifted from my shoulders. This weekend I was going to focus on Alain, Oliver, and myself.

Alain and I spent a quiet weekend together; just being around each other was enough. Sunday afternoon the phone rang. It was Chantal, telling me she was going back to the hospital, on the advice of her doctor. Her ankles were swollen. I could not believe it. She was home only for a few days and now she had to go back? She was fine with it. She actually said, "Mom, it's okay. I would rather be in the hospital, where they can look after me, than be at home." I told her how much I loved her and that I would see her at the hospital in the morning. I hated the fact Chantal had to return to the hospital. But when she told me she felt safer there, I was more at ease.

They kept Chantal almost two weeks, until they had her swelling under control. The doctors found out much later that Chantal's swelling was kept under control more easily when her medication for fluids was given through an IV, rather than in pill form. At last they told us she could go home. The doctor increased the dosage of one of her fluid pills and told her she had to watch her salt intake.

Chantal never slept well in ICU. We thought being in her own home, in her own environment, Chantal's sleep would improve. But it only got worse. Chantal was up half the night, and this made her more anxious and more miserable. I would find her pacing the floor in the middle of the night. Her lack of sleeping worried me tremendously. I knew Chantal needed her rest for her body to heal.

Once again she started retaining fluids, and her breathing was becoming difficult. She felt that her quality of life did not improve, even having gone through major surgery. She struggled to help with meals, the cleaning, and her exercises. But even these activities made her tired. I never knew what to expect on Monday mornings when I opened the front door. Sometimes she would greet me with a smile and say, "Hi, Mama." But more often than not, she would be in tears. She was exhausted from lack of sleep. This broke my heart.

Chantal had to visit the clinic in the hospital every two weeks for follow-up. Some days it would take forever to get her dressed. On one occasion Chantal did not get any sleep the night before. I had to cancel the appointment, because she was too weak to get dressed. Seeing her like this was discouraging. At this point I was also starting to feel that the surgery was all for nothing.

It was near the end of May, a time of leafy renewal. Yet Chantal saw none of it. She had already been admitted a few times for fluid retention. Her stay at the hospital always seemed to last two weeks. The doctors would change or increase her fluid pills, but it made no difference. She would be home for less than a week, then right back to the hospital. It never lasted long enough for her to get relief. This frustrated Chantal and made her more anxious. A few times I saw her crying.

Before the surgery Chantal was having difficulty breathing, but she was able to drive, go shopping, and do some simple chores around her house. Now she was barely eating, she rarely got dressed, and she was retaining more fluids. It took every bit of energy to have a shower. It was a trying time for all of us, but it was nothing compared to Chantal's experience. I could not begin to imagine what was in her mind. The look on her face showed sadness and discouragement. I began to feel Chantal was losing her will to live.

When I went home on the weekend, I would tell this to my husband. It saddened the both of us to see her go through this. We truly expected things would improve after surgery. The last time Chantal was admitted for swelling, the cardiologist explained why this was happening. The new valve that was inserted into the damaged part of the heart was not able to perform 100 percent effectively. The doctor had hoped the new valve would make a difference in Chantal's quality of life. Unfortunately, it was no better than before. Actually, things only got worse.

It was almost the end of June. Chantal had been in and out of the hospital for swelling several times. The surgeon was not quite sure what to do. I continued to do healings on Chantal and prayed things would get better. But Chantal's swelling would get worse, and again we would head back to the hospital. She seemed very different when she was there. Chantal told me she felt safe and that if anything were to happen, the nurses were around to help her. Chantal had so much more energy when her lungs were clearer. What were once small pleasures were now big victories. She would be able to do jigsaw puzzles, walk to the gift shop, and even to the cafeteria for no-salt fries!

It was a Monday morning, and I had returned to the hospital after another weekend at home. Chantal greeted me at the elevator doors. It was so nice to see her standing there. We exchanged big hugs and kisses and didn't care who saw us. We went back into her room to do my usual healing on her. I began to lay my hands on Chantal. My focus was directly on the heart area. I called on Jesus and archangels Michael and Raphael to send healing energy to my daughter. I always feel tingling and heat coming from my hands, but this time it felt so much more intense. I could actually feel the energy penetrating my hands and going directly into Chantal. She looked so relaxed. It was so powerful. After I finished she said Mom, "I saw Jesus, and the archangels Michael and Raphael."

Chantal had no idea I called on them to assist me in the healing. I asked, "How do you know it was them?"

She said, "Mom, I just know it." I understood that. This was the first time Chantal had experienced seeing Jesus. That moment I knew Chantal had felt a healing. She looked so peaceful. I was so happy for her, and truly grateful.

As a medium and a healer, I've found that sometimes when we do a healing on someone, it does not always come through as a physical healing, but instead as an emotional and spiritual one. This was what Chantal experienced that day.

That same morning, around ten o'clock, Chantal's surgeon came into the room and told us that there wasn't much else he could do for Chantal. She needed to be in the care of a cardiologist. Chantal told him she was not happy with her heart doctor and asked if he could recommend a new one. He told her he already had spoken to a heart specialist who would take her as a new patient. He would be in to see her that day.

Around 11:30 the new cardiologist walked into the room. He stood about six feet tall, had brown hair, and was wearing the typical hospital green pants and top. He said, "Hello, Chantal. I'm your new cardiologist, and I will be looking after you. I understand your health has not improved since the surgery."

"No, I feel worse. I'm still having difficulty breathing, and I keep retaining fluids."

He looked right at her and said, "I will do everything in my power to make you feel better." He was a big man but spoke softly. He was so caring and showed such compassion for my daughter. On this day we still had some faith that he would be able to help.

When he left the room, Chantal's eyes lit up. "Mom, I really like him; he is so nice."

"I like him too, dear." The doctor gave Chantal another sign of hope that she was finally going to have a chance for a better quality of life.

Chantal and I both remained very optimistic. She was smiling and feeling great. Her lungs were clear. She was strong enough to go for her physiotherapy treatment. Adam would come and visit after work, and Alissa would come in the evening and keep her company. Everything was going great. On the weekend Chantal would have her pass to go home and spend time with Adam and Spencer. I could return home to St. Catharines. This was getting to be our routine. It was the two-hour drive home I dreaded, but it was heaven to be home with my husband. Being around Alain and Oliver the cat gave me immense solace, as I was starting to feel drained by everything that was happening. Yet these peaceful weekends flew by without mercy.

Monday morning it was time for me to return to London and be with Chantal. Adam and Alissa had brought her back to the hospital Sunday night. My daughter knew I would always leave my house around eight. It usually took two hours, depending on the traffic, but somehow Chantal always seemed to know exactly when to walk to the elevators to greet me. These times were few and far between, only when her lungs were clear. We treasured these moments. Although it was wonderful being home, I was truly grateful for this time with Chantal.

The doctors were starting on their rounds, so we thought we should return to her room. There we met her new cardiologist. "Hello, Chantal. How was your weekend at home?"

"It was great. I went with Adam and some of my friends to Summerfest in the park. I even ate a bag of popcorn with no salt."

"I'm glad you had fun." After examining Chantal he said, "I have decided for the next two weeks we will be repeating some of the tests you already had and performing new ones. We need to see if you qualify to be on the heart transplant list." Chantal and I both looked at each other. There had been no mention of this earlier on. I was shocked to hear this news. Chantal looked relieved and very excited. She was going to have a new heart.

The doctor told us that besides all the necessary tests, Chantal would once again have to speak with a counselor, a psychologist, a nutritionist, and an occupational therapist. She didn't care at this point; she was going to do whatever it took. Even after having had major surgery almost three months before, she was determined to go through yet another to feel better. That takes courage. I was never so proud of my daughter. When he left the room, Chantal and I gave each other the biggest hug. She got out of bed and immediately started dancing with joy. I was so happy for her. She grabbed the phone to call Adam at work and give him the great news. He was just as excited and told her he would come up right after work. We knew Alissa was coming up for a visit at lunch. We were going to surprise her then. I had to wait until four o'clock to reach Alain at home.

Chantal couldn't wait to see Alissa. The minute she walked in the room, she told her the great news. "I'm getting a new heart."

"That's wonderful. I'm so happy for you." They hugged each other. Alissa said, "We can have a fundraiser for you, Chantal." We thought that was a great idea. We took a piece of paper and started to plan the event, what games we would have, the menu, who would attend, what we would charge. We thought of everything that was going to make this party a success. Thanks to Alissa, we had something good and positive to focus on besides the new heart. The last three months had been so discouraging.

It was 4:15, and by then Alain would be home from work. I always called him around that time to give him our daily updates on Chantal. That day he would have no idea what we were about to tell him. Chantal wanted to be the first to give him the exciting news. When she heard his voice say, "Hello," she replied, "Al, you won't believe it. I'm getting a new heart. We're going to throw a big party for me."

"I'm so happy for you, Chantal. I love you."

"I love you, Al. Here is Mom." She was so wound up she couldn't talk.

When I got on the phone with him, he was crying. He was thrilled. "God has answered our prayers."

"I believe it."

"I love you both so much."

"I love you too."

"I wish I could be there with you."

"I know, dear. I would like that too."

"I will call you tomorrow. Have a good night, dear."

"I will."

"Goodbye, Louise."

"Bye, dear."

For the next few days, Chantal bounced back and forth doing the tests. One of them came back showing that Chantal's kidneys were not functioning at 100 percent capacity. I was chilled to my bones. But the doctor assured us that this was very common in these cases. Chantal saw that I still looked worried. She tried to reassure me. "Mom, don't worry; it's going to be okay. You heard what the doctor said." Once again, she tried to make me feel better. It was she who showed no sign of fear. I did see Chantal's nurse practitioner from the clinic on the ward and asked her about it. She told me the exact same thing. I stopped worrying.

During the next two weeks, Chantal spoke to a nutritionist who explained her dietary restrictions. The therapist explained the different exercises she would need to do to strengthen her arms and legs. The counselor helped Chantal fill out the necessary papers for financial support. Chantal had used up all her unemployment insurance benefits. This was great news; she had been so worried about her finances. The psychologist worked with Chantal to help her deal with certain emotional issues. There were certain people and times in her life that Chantal needed to work on forgiving, including herself, and let it go. That doesn't happen overnight, but the few times Chantal saw the doctor helped a great deal. We also met with the hospital heart transplant coordinator. His job is to find and match a heart to a patient.

He explained to us that after all the testing if Chantal qualified, she would be put on a list for a new heart. Qualifying also depended on the severity of the patient's need. It could take hours, days, months, even a year to find a match. Once she was on the list, she would have to carry a beeper on her person at all times, so they could page her in the event they had a heart. As soon as the beeper went off, she would have to go directly to the hospital.

It was important to ensure that Chantal understood everything required of her before and after the surgery. Chantal had been feeling wonderful since the doctors told her about the heart transplant. She had a good appetite, and her lungs were clear, making it easier for her to breathe.

The Friday of the second week was the thirteenth. Around 1:30 in the afternoon, the heart transplant coordinator came into the room and announced it was official: she was on the transplant list. Chantal and I were so excited. This was definitely a time for celebration. Now it was just a matter of waiting for a new heart to be available. He would be back later to give her a beeper. The nurse then came in with more good news: Chantal was being discharged. She could go home.

Chantal was thrilled about the whole thing, but in the car on the way home she said, "Mom, what if it takes a long time for them to find a heart for me? I can't keep living like this. The heart transplant coordinator did say it could take up to a year. I don't think I can wait that long."

"Chantal, God will take care of you. You need to have faith and trust that everything is going to work out." We were both silent for a few minutes. She couldn't wait to get home. Adam was waiting for Chantal and greeted her with open arms. She then picked up Spencer and gave him lots of kisses. It was time for me to leave for the weekend. I hugged and kissed her and told her how much I loved her and began my drive to St. Catharines.

CHAPTER 7

Another Chance at Life

It was good being in my own house with Alain, relaxing and sharing our emotions, knowing that Chantal would have a chance at a healthier life. On Sunday afternoon, around three o'clock, I happened to be on the phone talking to a friend when Alain came running downstairs crying, "They have a heart for Chantal!"

"What!"

"They have a heart for Chantal."

"Oh my God! I can't believe it. It's only been a few days." I said to the person on the phone, "I have to hang up; they found a heart for my daughter." I hung up the phone, embraced Alain, and ran upstairs to get ready. I couldn't believe how quickly this happened. It was a miracle. We were out of the house within half an hour.

In the meantime, Chantal had gone directly to the hospital. Thankfully, Alain and I arrived just in time. Adam and Alissa were sitting with Chantal by her bedside. She was very happy to see us. "I'm so glad you made it. I was afraid I was going to be in surgery before you got here."

"I couldn't believe it when Alain told me you called. That was fast."

"I know. I was making spaghetti sauce when my beeper went off. Adam and I couldn't believe it either. I had to turn everything off and leave for the hospital."

We did not have a chance to spend much time with her. Soon the orderly came to take her for surgery. I held Chantal's hand and kept kissing her. All I could think about was how brave my daughter was, going through even more major surgery. I told her I was sending in Raphael, the archangel for healing, to be by her side and not to fear. Chantal looked pretty calm, considering what she was about to face. We all told her we loved her and kissed her as they wheeled her away.

Rushing to get to the hospital, Alain and I did not have a chance to call John or Thomas. I waited for the doctor to come in and speak with us before I phoned. We were sitting in the waiting room when the surgeon came. He introduced himself. "Hello. I will be performing the operation on Chantal."

"We have not received the heart yet. When it arrives, I will examine it and make sure it's healthy and compatible before we place it into Chantal."

"Can you tell us where the heart is coming from and who is the donor?"

"The heart comes from a female older than Chantal, and it's from the Hamilton area. The surgery takes about ten hours.

We're hoping to start around eight o'clock tonight. After the surgery I will come and talk to you."

"Thank you, doctor."

As soon as the doctor left the room, I called John and Thomas. They were both quite shocked. I told them the transplant would take about ten hours. It was probably a good idea to come in the morning. That way at least they would get some sleep. I knew sleep was going to be out of the question for Alain, Alissa, Adam, and me. We agreed we would all see each other in the morning.

We were given a private room to wait in during the operation. There were two couches, a television, and a table with chairs. There was also a deck of cards, puzzles, and magazines on the table to pass the time. We were all so very grateful. This was so much more comfortable than sitting on chairs in the busy waiting room. We knew it was going to be a long night.

Besides Alain and me, Adam, and Alissa, Chantal had five other wonderful supportive friends there, waiting to see her through surgery. She was blessed to have such good friends. We talked about how brave and courageous Chantal was to be willing to go through another major surgery in order to feel better. We shared stories of happy times with Chantal, how she was an inspiration to so many people, how her infectious laughter would make us all laugh. It was a great time for reminiscing.

Alain and I needed to stretch our legs, so we decided to go downstairs to the chapel to say a prayer for Chantal and send her healings. It is very stressful when a loved one is being operated on. You worry and you fear the unknown. Going to pray gave me a sense of peace. While some of us were able to get a few hours of sleep, I stayed awake the whole night. Having no idea what time they started the operation, we had no idea when they were going to be finished.

By eight o'clock in the morning, John and Thomas arrived. I told them we still had not heard anything. Their presence would make Chantal very happy. She had not seen her father and brother for a few months. We were all showing signs of restlessness and fatigue. I was beginning to worry that something might have gone wrong. We dared not leave the room in case the doctors came in with news. Waiting, we watched the clock and figured that surely it couldn't be much longer.

An hour and a half later, we were all deeply tired and feared this delay. What was happening? Finally, the doctor came into the room and told us they did not start the surgery until eleven o'clock the night before. He had run into a few complications. When he cut open Chantal's chest, he noticed her left lung had managed to attach itself to her heart. They had to be very careful to detach it before they could remove the heart. That was why it took so long. He assured us that other than that, the surgery had gone well. He asked us to give the nurses about an hour to do their job, and then we could go see her. We all gave a sigh of relief, and I thanked God.

While we were waiting to go in and see Chantal, I couldn't help but think, *Chantal was wheeled away around 6:30, and the surgery did not start until eleven. I can't even begin to imagine what was going on in her mind. Waiting that long, not knowing if the heart was going to be healthy or not or even having the surgery must have been torture. How brave and courageous she was to have endured all of this pain and stress.* She never complained or ever talked about it.

I couldn't sit still. Having to wait only brought back memories from three months ago. Here we were, repeating the same thing. My energy was starting to be depleted. It was time to see Chantal. We asked the nurse whether it was okay if Alain, her dad and brother, and I could all go in together. She agreed it was fine, as long as we did not stay very long. Adam, Alissa, and a few other friends could go in later.

I was amazed at how great Chantal looked, considering the tubes that were connected to her and what she had just gone through. She looked far better than after her first surgery. She couldn't talk because of the breathing tube, but she was alert and happy to see all of us, especially her dad and brother. She looked directly at her father and brother. Her eyes lit up, and, even with the tube in her mouth, I knew she was smiling. She was especially glad to see the two of them. We all told her how much we loved her and how proud we were. She responded by blinking.

We couldn't stay long, as we had to share time with the others. The private room was available to us all day, so we picked up some lunch and ate there. We sat and talked about Chantal and how strong and brave she was. We talked about all Chantal endured and what an inspiration she was to so many people, and also how much spunk Chantal packed in such a tiny frame. Talking about her made the atmosphere in the room very happy, pleasant, and positive. But then again, when you saw or thought of Chantal, this was how she always made you feel. We were all able to see her one more time that day. She was looking very tired. We said our usual good-byes, gave her kisses, and told her we'd be back.

Chantal, at twenty years old, on her Disney cruise

Chantal, age twenty-four, at our family barbecue

First Christmas in her new townhouse, age twenty-eight

Chantal's last Christmas, at twenty-nine years old

The next morning, we were able to see Chantal for only a few minutes. It was difficult for her to communicate because of the breathing tube. With effort, she was able to convey that her left foot was sore. When I pulled the sheet off, I noticed her foot looked bruised, swollen, and purple in different spots. I was getting concerned. *Was the new heart causing this problem?*

In the ICU visiting was not permitted much before eleven in the morning. The doctor did his rounds earlier in the morning, so I never had the opportunity to speak with him. The nurses were always very caring and made sure that if I had any questions, they would mention that to the doctor. This bruising was a big concern to me. Later that day the doctor happened to be by the nurse's station. The attending nurse must have spoken to him, because as soon as the surgeon saw me, he approached me. He explained to me that after a heart transplant, there can be signs of poor circulation and that it should improve in a few days.

I began to massage Chantal's foot to alleviate some of the swelling and pain and also to help bring back the circulation. During the day, we did the massage every time we were in the room with Chantal, and Alissa worked on it in the evening, giving Chantal much relief.

Over the next few days the colour did improve, and she was getting better circulation. By Tuesday morning they had removed her breathing tube, and Chantal was now, happily, able to speak. I had to ask her, "How does it feel to have another person's heart inside you? You know how they say people have certain cravings or want to do something they never did before."

"I really don't feel any different. Maybe it's too soon."

It was hard for Chantal to lie in the same position for any length of time; her back would get very sore. It was difficult to make her comfortable, what with all the tubes. With the help of the nurse, we would adjust her position to bring her some relief. We continued to visit as much as we could. We could never stay very long; we did not want to wear Chantal down. We usually did all the talking, or we just sat there and kept her company. She did not mind that at all. Chantal's rest was important for her recovery.

Adam and I left to get some rest ourselves. Alain had to return to St. Catharines. He called me around 9:30 to tell me he was home and that he loved me. I told Alain I loved him and wished him a good-night. About eleven Alissa called to tell us that while she was visiting, Chantal was having difficulty breathing on her own. The doctor had to put a breathing tube back in. I felt so bad for my daughter. I knew how much she hated having this in her throat. I tried not to worry, as the doctor had told her this was normal after having a heart transplant. That night I sent Chantal healings and prayed that she would improve quickly, just as she had done in the past.

I did not mind Alain having to leave; there were responsibilities at home that needed to be looked after. Besides Adam, I had Chantal's dad, John, to keep me company during the day. We were both able to visit at the same time but could only stay for short visits. Chantal was happy to have her dad there. I continued to massage Chantal's foot, and it seemed to improve considerably. Chantal was still experiencing discomfort in her back. We just kept readjusting her position in the bed. That seemed to make it more bearable.

Without the breathing tube, it was easier for Chantal to speak. But the rest of the time, there were periods she still had to use an alphabet board. Wednesday was one of those days. She tried talking with this tube inside her throat; of course, I couldn't understand what she was trying to convey. She then got very frustrated. When I told her I did not comprehend what she was trying to say, she tried to spell it out on the board. Even then there were times I didn't know. She then got upset and irritated with me. I just let Chantal vent. If I was her sounding board, it was okay with me.

Thursday morning before I could see Chantal, the nurse approached me. "Louise, it is very important for Chantal to receive nourishment. The only way is for us to insert a feeding tube. We have already tried to talk her into it, and she was adamantly against the whole thing. Is there any way you can convince her? She needs to realize how important it is to gain her strength back."

"I understand. When Chantal had her valve replaced she told me that under no circumstances would she allow the doctor to put in a feeding tube. This will not be easy, but I will do my best."

Chantal never explained why she was so stubborn about this whole ordeal. After the first surgery there was no need for it. Chantal was drinking her protein shakes and eating, so I never brought up the issue. Having to convince Chantal to have this procedure done was not something I was looking forward to, but I knew it was necessary.

When I pulled the curtain, I noticed once again that the doctor had removed Chantal's breathing tube. That was a good thing. I thought, *Maybe this will make what I am about to do a little easier.* I gave her a big kiss and asked her how she was feeling. I could see by the look on her face that she was not pleased. I started talking to her about Spencer sitting on my lap while I watched television, and how he slept with me the night before. Also, that her dad was coming up to visit later that day. That seemed to change her mood a little. I had to wait for the right timing, and then I came out with it.

"Chantal, the nurse wanted me to talk to you about the feeding tube."

She got so angry, she said to the nurse, "Get her out of here; I don't want to talk to her. I am not going to have them put that tube in me. Mom, leave. I don't want to see you right now." She was very upset. I thought it best to leave her alone. I told her I would be back later.

I did not take it personally. Chantal was going through so much, and I did not blame her for not wanting this. But how could I make her understand this was for her own good? I went down to the chapel and prayed to God for his guidance. I sent prayers of healing, gave her plenty of time to rest, and went back to see her after lunch. I guess Chantal had by then had time to reflect on what had happened.

When she saw me she said, "Mom, I am so sorry for what I said earlier. I didn't mean it."

"I know, dear. I understand, and it's okay. We are all concerned about you getting enough nutrition. That is why I mentioned it." At this point she still had not agreed to have the procedure done. I could see she did not want to discuss it any further. Maybe Chantal needed more time to think about it. I dropped the subject for that moment, and I began to massage her foot to relieve some of the pain. Leaving her that night, I prayed she would consent to having the feeding tube put in.

Once again my prayers were answered. Around ten that night the phone rang, and the voice on the other end said, "Hi, Louise. It's Alissa. Chantal has agreed to allow the doctors to put the tube in."

"Oh, that's wonderful news! What made her change her mind?"

"I told her if she wanted to get better, she needed to get some nourishment in her to gain her strength back."

"Thank you so much, Alissa, for being there and convincing her. I am truly grateful to you."

"There is something else I have to tell you. The doctor had to hook Chantal up to a kidney dialysis machine."

When I heard those words, I felt sick to my stomach. I was shocked. "Why, what wrong with her kidneys?"

"Don't worry; the doctor told me this was normal under the circumstances."

I tried to be positive, but all I could think about was that my daughter now had kidney failure. With a lump in my throat, I asked, "How is Chantal doing through all of this?"

"She seems to be in good spirits."

"That's good. I can't believe it; first it's the feeding tube, and now this. How much more can she endure?"

"Chantal is strong; she will pull through this."

"Thanks again, Alissa. I am going to let you go now." I couldn't say much more.

I felt so sad for my daughter. I did not want to think the worst, but it seemed like it was one thing after another. I wanted to jump in the car and head straight to the hospital to put my arms around my daughter and comfort her. But I knew I would have to wait until morning.

Adam was in the other bedroom watching television. I now had to inform him of this news. "Adam, that was Alissa on the phone." He immediately came out of the room. "Chantal has agreed to let the doctor put in the feeding tube, but now they have to hook her up to a kidney dialysis machine. Alissa assured me the doctor told her it was normal after a heart transplant."

"How is Chantal taking it?"

"Alissa said she was in good spirits. You know how Chantal is; she always tries to be brave and never wants us to worry about her."

He had a look of concern on his face. "It seems that things are getting worse instead of better."

"We have to believe it will get better."

"Thanks, Louise."

Neither one of us felt much like talking. I know I felt discouraged; as for Adam, he was going through his own emotions. I felt bad not only for my daughter but for Adam as well. I went back to my room and sent prayers and healings to Adam and my beautiful, beleaguered daughter.

I did not get much sleep that night. Friday morning I woke up feeling pretty drained. I hurried to get ready, and off I went to see Chantal. When I arrived, I expected to see the feeding tube in her nose. It wasn't there. I thought maybe they hadn't had a chance to insert it yet. However, I did notice a couple of bottles of the protein drink on Chantal's table.

"Mom, before you say anything, I promised the doctor I would drink my shakes." He had agreed to hold off on the tube.

"I am so happy for you, dear. I know how much you hated the idea. I see the nurse cleaned you up and washed your hair."

"Yes, I feel so much better."

Taking the brush, I offered to unsnarl her hair. I was very gentle, careful not to hurt her or catch the brush on the tubes. The fragrance of her hair was so wonderful as I leaned over to kiss her forehead. I would have loved to hold her tight, but I couldn't. The tubes were preventing me from doing so. I would have changed places with her in a minute, just so she would not have to endure more pain. It broke my heart to see my beautiful baby this way.

The days seemed to go quickly, especially with her dad, John, to keep me company, but they were mentally and emotionally exhausting. Adam too was so supportive. He would work all day and then come to the hospital to visit. I could tell he really cared about Chantal and was concerned about her health. He stayed with her throughout the good times and the bad. I am so grateful to him and thank him for loving her this way.

That afternoon when Chantal was resting, I happened to see her nurse practitioner and asked her why Chantal needed to be hooked up to the kidney dialysis machine. She told me the same thing Alissa had told me. It was a normal procedure after a heart transplant. I guess I needed to be reassured that Chantal was not going into kidney failure.

On Friday, John, Adam, and I had a good visit. Chantal was free of the feeding and breathing tubes. The circulation in her foot had improved considerably. She was in such happy spirits. I felt such peace seeing her like this. My sister Ginette had called earlier that day to speak with Chantal. She wanted to come up and visit on Saturday. Alain had already told Chantal he was coming to see her on Sunday. She was really looking forward to their visit.

It seemed like a good time for me to go home for the weekend and relax. I asked her if it was okay for me to leave. "Mom, go home and get some rest. Aunt Ginette, Uncle Sandy, and Cousin Jennifer are coming to see me on Saturday, and Al is coming on Sunday. I will be fine."

"Are you sure? I can stay if you want me to."

"No, please go."

"Do you want me to come back on Sunday with Al?"

"No, I want him all to myself."

"Okay, if that's what you want." Knowing this made it so much easier for me to leave her side. I gave her my usual big kiss. "I love you so much."

"I love you too, Mom." You can never hear it enough. Chantal never had a problem telling people she loved them. It was very important to her that everyone know this.

John leaned over to kiss her good-bye and told her he would see her on Monday. By six that evening we were on the road heading for home. I did feel great comfort knowing that her family was going to visit her the next day. Even though I couldn't wait to get home, the two-hour ride seemed more pleasant.

I had a good sleep that night. I felt more rested than I had in months. Saturday morning as soon as I got out of bed, I phoned the hospital to see how Chantal was feeling and how she spent the night. The nurse told me Chantal was sitting up watching television and that she was drinking her protein shakes. That was music to my ears. I asked the nurse to tell her I was so happy for her and that I loved her. The nurse repeated my message to Chantal. I heard her in the background saying how much she loved me and that she was looking forward to seeing the family that day. I can't begin to tell you how good that made me feel. I breathed a sigh of relief, wishing her a wonderful day. Alain was very excited when I told him he couldn't wait to see her.

On Sunday morning Alain left for the hospital around nine to get there in time for visiting hours. As much as I wanted to go with him, I honoured Chantal's wishes to allow the two of them time alone. He had planned to spend the whole day with Chantal. He was a little early, so they asked him to wait before he went in. Finally, the nurse gave him permission to see Chantal, but she told him he could stay only for a few minutes, that Chantal needed her rest.

The nurse explained to Alain that Chantal had a rough night, didn't get any sleep, and wasn't feeling very well. She had begun to have difficulty with breathing, and her leg was bothering her. He agreed he wouldn't stay long. Even though Chantal was not feeling well, her eyes lit up when she saw him. He leaned over to kiss her on the forehead and told her he loved her. He also told her she needed her rest and that he would see her later on. She was so exhausted that she nodded it was all right for him to leave.

While at home I decided to call my sister to see how her visit went with Chantal the day before. They had been allowed to stay only for a few minutes, but Chantal was still delighted to see them. My niece Jennifer told me that Chantal asked each of them how they were. "Aunt Louise, I couldn't believe it. After everything that Chantal has gone through, she is asking us how we are doing." Jennifer told me she had tears in her eyes when Chantal spoke and was so glad they went to see her. I started to cry after I hung up the phone. I said to myself, *My God, what a brave young woman she is. I am so proud of her.* Chantal was more concerned about how other people were doing than talking about her pain.

Alain was still waiting for permission to go back to be with Chantal when Adam arrived. Around two o'clock they were allowed back in to see her. Chantal's breathing was getting worse, and she had no circulation in the leg that was bothering her. When they walked in, the doctor was explaining to Chantal that to help her breathing he would have to insert a needle in her side to draw the fluids from her lung. Chantal gave the surgeon permission to do the procedure. After the doctor left, Adam talked with Chantal while Alain massaged her foot. Once again they were in there for only about ten minutes when the nurse asked them to leave the room. But before they did, Alain looked at Chantal and said, "Today is the beginning of a new life." Alain had no idea why he said this to her.

He told me that the way she stared at him, it was as though she understood he was giving her soul permission to leave. She smiled and that was the last time they saw her alive.

I was still at home when, around 5:30, Alain called me from the hospital. "Hi, dear, it's me. Chantal has been having some difficulty breathing again. The doctor is going to put a needle in her side to remove the fluid from her lung. This will help her breathe easier. She told the doctor to go ahead and do it."

"Is she all right?"

"I could see she was having problems. Adam and I could only see her for a few minutes. I don't know any more than what I have already told you."

"Should I come up to the hospital?"

"Wait until I call you back with more news."

"Okay, dear, I love you."

"I love you too."

I hung up the phone, sat down, and started to cry. *Oh, God! This can't be happening. How much more can she take? Please, God, take care of my baby. She has gone through so much. I was so scared I wanted so much to be with her.* Waiting for Alain to call me back was making me more frightened and more nervous. I needed to meditate to calm myself and send healing to Chantal. I did not want to think the worst but decided to go and get my bag ready just in case.

Finally, around seven o'clock, the phone rang. It was Alain. "Louise, I just spoke to the doctor. He tried putting the needle in Chantal's side, but she started to bleed. They have to take her into the operating room to do the procedure. I think you should pack a suitcase and get to the hospital as soon as you can. Bring me some clothes too."

"I'm on my way."

Not knowing how long we were going to be gone, I had to call my friend Cathy to keep an eye on Oliver. I explained the situation and told her I would call her with any news. She agreed to watch the cat. I threw some clothes in for Alain and was out the door by 7:30.

I had a two-hour drive ahead of me. It had started to rain, and it was dismal outside. I prayed to Michael, my protector, and to God to guide me and get me there safely and take care of Chantal. I had been driving only a short while when it started to pour. I could hardly see the road. The traffic inched forward. I was so scared. When I finished praying, a strong feeling came over me, and I knew Chantal was no longer with us.

I am a Clairsentient and as a medium, a lot of my messages come through as a feeling. At that moment I felt strongly that my daughter's soul had crossed over.

As a mother, for one quick instant, I thought it was my ego bringing on these negative thoughts. *No, Louise, when you get to the hospital, Alain will tell you that everything went well, Chantal is in recovery, and we will be able to see her later.* As soon as I had that thought, I felt like there was something on my lap. I thought it was the weight of my shoulder purse, but it was off to the side. I even moved my hand up and down and side to side to see if I could feel anything. There was absolutely nothing on my lap. It was like someone or something was sitting on my lap. I felt I was not alone. It was a peaceful feeling. Shortly after, the rain subsided.

I arrived at the hospital around 9:30. Since it was after hours, the front doors were locked, and a sign said to go to the emergency entrance. As I started to walk towards that door, I saw Adam coming down the hall. I thought he was going outside for a cigarette. When he saw me he ran and put his arms around me and started to sob. "I'm so sorry, I'm so sorry. Chantal is gone."

I began to cry. In my mind I was saying, *No, she can't be. No! Oh God, no!* I felt such emptiness. "Adam, no, she can't be."

"Chantal is gone, Louise. Everybody is in the private room waiting for you." That was the same room they had given us when she had her transplant.

When I opened the door to go in, Alain got up and held me in his arms. Crying he whispered, "Chantal is gone. She's gone."

"Alain, she can't be."

"Chantal suffered enough. It was time for her to go. I know that she fought all she could." I looked around the room. There was complete silence. Alissa and some of Chantal's other friends looked so sad. They had lost their good friend.

This was not possible. I felt so empty inside. My beautiful baby girl was gone. I sat down. Alain started to tell me what the two doctors had told them. "The surgeon told us when they tried to insert the needle to drain the fluids, there were complications. Chantal started bleeding heavily, and they couldn't stop it. He told us they did everything they could to try and save her. One of them had blood all over his shoes. Louise, I believe the doctors did all they could. They both looked so sad having to bring us this horrible news."

"I believe him."

I knew in my heart that Chantal had decided that enough was enough. Her frail little body couldn't take the pain anymore, and she had decided that it was time to go back to her Creator, where her soul would live on in peace and no more pain.

I needed some time to process all of this, and I dreaded what I had to do next. I had to call Chantal's dad, her brother, and my sister Ginette and give them the news. I tried both John and Thomas but couldn't get a hold of either one. I then phoned my sister. I was so nervous I couldn't find her number on my cell phone. Finally the voice on the other end said hello.

"Ginette, it's me."

"What's wrong?"

"Chantal is gone."

"Oh no, Louise. I am so sorry. What happened?"

"Chantal had problems with her breathing. They tried to insert a needle to drain the fluids, and there was heavy bleeding, and other complications. The doctors did all they could to save her."

"I know there is nothing I can say to make you feel better. If there is anything Sandy and I can do to help you, please let us know. I will call the family for you."

"Thanks. That would be a great help I don't know how long we will be in London. I will call you as soon as I know more."

"Love you."

"Love you too."

I then had to call Cathy. "Hi, Cathy. It's me. Chantal didn't make it."

"Oh, no! Oh, God. Louise, I am so sorry."

"I have no idea how long we will be in London."

"Don't worry. I'll look after Oliver."

"I'll explain everything another time." I was using my cell phone, and the battery was getting low.

"Call me as soon as you can."

"I will." As I was getting off the phone, a nurse came in to tell us we could see Chantal and spend our last moments with her if we wanted to. Alain, Adam, and I chose to. We needed to. Her friends chose to remember her when she was alive.

On the way there I felt like I was in a hurry to see her, as though Chantal was going to be alive when we got there. I felt this was all a dream, that she was in recovery waiting to see us. When the nurse opened the door to the room, her lifeless body just lay there. Her face was swollen. I hardly recognized her. She did not look like my beautiful baby. As soon as Adam saw her, he started to cry. He turned and fled the room. He could not see her this way.

The nurse told us we could stay as long as we wanted. Seeing her lying there, I now understood that she was really gone. I can't explain it: I was heartbroken that she was no longer alive, and yet I had a sense of peace knowing she was no longer suffering. Alain and I sat down beside her. I kissed her on the forehead and held her hand.

We spoke to her as though she was still alive, telling her how much we loved her and what a wonderful daughter she was. I told her it was okay that she decided to go back home to be with God. We understood she had given it her all, and now it was her time to go. We told her we would truly miss her beautiful smile. Alain asked her to be around us and to watch over us. The rest of the time we sat there quietly, just watching her. We knew this was going to be the last time to ever see her again. I have no idea how long we were in the room, but I knew when it was the right time to leave her side. Alain and I leaned over and gave Chantal one final kiss.

Before we left the room, I turned and took one final look at my daughter; then Alain and I walked out of the room holding hands. At that very moment, I felt at peace, and I knew with God's and Chantal's help we were all going to get through this.

When we got back to the private room, everyone was still pretty quiet. I had to go and speak with the nurse to ask them what was going to happen to Chantal's body. Chantal had registered to donate her organs and body to science. I wanted to make sure they were aware of that. The nurse from ICU wasn't able to help me, but she did say she would have someone from the hospital get in touch with me.

It was around eleven; time to leave the hospital. Adam had decided to stay with Alissa and their other friends. I understood he needed to be with them throughout this trying time. Alain and I left to go get some rest. The ride back to Chantal's place was about twenty minutes from the hospital. Halfway home my cell phone rang. It was the nurse. "Mrs. Michaud, we spoke earlier about Chantal donating her organs and body to science. Unfortunately, we cannot use them because of her illnesses and surgeries. You will have to make the necessary arrangements to have her body picked up at the hospital."

"What about her eyes? Can she at least donate her eyes?"

Chantal always said, "Mom, if my organs are of no value, then at least I can donate my eyes to help someone see."

"I will have someone from the Foundation get in touch with you."

"Thank you."

Alain and I had just had time to get upstairs and sit and relax when my cell phone rang again. "Mrs. Michaud."

"Yes, this is she."

"I'm calling from the Foundation. I would like to offer you my condolences. I am so sorry for your loss. How old was your daughter?"

"She was twenty-nine years old."

"She was very young."

"I understand Chantal wanted to donate her corneas. I will need to ask you several questions before the Foundation can commit to using them."

This was not the best time to answer all her questions, but I knew how important this was to my daughter. I felt I needed to do this for her.

The young lady proceeded to ask me questions about Chantal's surgeries and illnesses. How old was she when she got sick? What illnesses and surgeries did she have? It was necessary to know the background of the donor. We were on the phone for a good half hour, as it was important that they receive all the facts. I know that certain organs have to be removed within minutes and transported as soon as possible, but I wasn't sure about the eyes. The person I was speaking to assured me that in the case of the eyes, the timing is different and that they would remove them either that night or early Monday morning. She also told me that could they use not only the corneas, but also the tissues around the eyes. I told them how pleased Chantal would be that she would make a difference in another person's life.

All of this was a lot to take in. I was completely drained of all my energy when I hung up the phone. I looked at Alain. "They are going to take Chantal's corneas and tissues either tonight or early tomorrow morning."

"That's good news. Chantal would be happy."

"Yes, I am very grateful. We have to make arrangements to have Chantal's body removed from the hospital." Chantal and I had talked about it, and she always said she wanted to be cremated.

"Louise, we're both exhausted. Let's try and get some sleep and talk about it in the morning."

Alain decided he was going to watch a little television to help him unwind. Poor Spencer felt lost without Chantal. He was moping around, going back and forth from Chantal's bed to the living room. I went to lie down and tried to get some rest. I started to pray and ask for guidance. *God, take care of my baby for me. I really need you right now. If you can help us get through this, I would be so grateful.* That was all it took. Within seconds it came to me. Rather than have Chantal's body picked up by our local funeral home, I would have her body cremated in London and bring the ashes back home for her memorial service. All we had to do was find a crematory in the London area. I got up, ran into the living room, and told Alain. He thought that was a great idea. He would look in the phone book when he got up the next day.

Monday morning my husband took out the phone book, and guess where the pages opened up to: Crematory. "Louise, come here. You won't believe this. I grabbed the book off the shelf, and when I placed it on the table, this is where it fell open." I looked down, and there they were: the names of crematories in the London area.

I said to Alain, "Chantal is definitely making things easy for us." We both believed it. I called to set our appointment for ten o'clock. Once the paperwork was done, our contact told us, they would look after transporting Chantal's body from the hospital, and we could return Wednesday to pick up her ashes. Chantal could not have made it any easier for us.

By noon we were heading back to St. Catharines with my daughter's cat, Spencer. I felt so sad for the little guy. You could tell he knew there was something going on. He just wasn't himself. The ride home was two hours long, and Spencer cried all the way. Chantal and Spencer had such a wonderful bond. She loved him so much, and he loved her. Now he would never see her again. He would have to get used to living in a strange home with our cat, Oliver, who would want no part of him.

CHAPTER 8

Communication from the Other Side

W hen Alain and I returned home, I couldn't sit still, so
we decided to make some of the arrangements for
Chantal's service. This was all new to me. I had no idea how
many people would be coming or what size room would be
needed. We both knew Chantal had many friends, and there
would be quite a few if everyone showed up. There was a
funeral home that was able to accommodate such a large
group. They were wonderful and helpful during this hard
time. They looked after every detail and made it much easier
for us.

Alain and I decided to have the memorial the following
Monday. This would give plenty of time for family and friends
to come from out of town. We also needed a minister to officiate
at Chantal's service. The only person that I wanted for this task
was my dear friend and mentor, Anita. She was the wonderful
lady whose spiritual development class I had attended. I called

her from the funeral home, and she told me it would be an honour to do this for me.

Anita had met Chantal only a few brief times. She did not know too much about her, except for what I had told her. To be able to talk about Chantal on a more personal level at the service, Anita came over that night to ask questions and to get the feel of my daughter. My friend Cathy happened to be visiting, helping me put some pictures together.

We began to tell Anita what a wonderful, loving, caring spirit Chantal was. We talked about how courageous she was to be willing to go through two major surgeries within three months of each other in order to have a better quality of life. How strong and determined Chantal was to get back to work so soon after her stroke.

We told her how she lived her life to the fullest. How she did things beyond our expectations during her illnesses. How she rarely complained when she was in pain. She always put everyone else's feelings before hers. We shared some funny stories and talked about her wonderful sense of humour and her great laughter. How Chantal was an inspiration to so many people. Everyone who knew Chantal loved her. With all the information we gave Anita, she was able to understand and know the real Chantal.

"You have given me a lot of good information. When I get home tonight I will do a meditation and see what else I can feel from Chantal. I will let you know if I receive a message."

"That would be great, Anita. Thank you so much."

"Tomorrow night I am having an Angel meditation class; I will do it in honour of Chantal. Would you and Alain like to attend?"

"We would love to. Thanks again." We all hugged each other and said good-bye.

In this particular meditation you call on an angel to come and take you on a journey to a favourite place. You get into a deep state of meditation. You converse with the angel and ask it to come before you, give you a name. You ask it to bring you a gift and a message. You wait for the answers and see what special place it will take you. It is a wonderful experience.

On Tuesday morning I received an email from Anita saying that Chantal had come through Monday night with a message for Alain, Adam, and me. I will share only what Chantal said for me: "Mom, it is more beautiful over here than you can ever imagine." As I was reading it, I burst into tears. This message from my daughter brought me such peace and comfort. I knew she was happier and no longer in pain. I was grateful that she came through for Anita. When Chantal was alive she always thought of others and knew how to make people feel good, and now, so soon after her passing, she was still thinking of us. What a wonderful gift to receive.

John, Chantal's dad, who had volunteered to do the obituary for the newspaper, stopped in for a visit that day, as did my brother-in-law Tom. We had to bring the obituary to the funeral home as soon as possible to get it to the paper on time. John and Tom both wanted to come with us, to see where the services were going to be held. After making a few changes to the obituary, the four of us drove off. John and Tom were both very pleased with the funeral home we chose. They thought it was perfect for the memorial.

Alain and I really looked forward to this evening. Once everyone had arrived, Anita began doing the guided meditation. Within minutes I felt my daughter's presence in the room. I actually felt her on my right side. I became so emotional, I started to cry. I could no longer hear Anita's voice as she was guiding everyone through the meditation. I started talking to Chantal. *Oh, honey. I know you're here; I can feel you. I love you and miss you so much. Thank you for your message; it brought me such peace. I know you are okay and no longer in pain. I know you will watch over us.*

Feeling my daughter's energy around me was wonderful and emotional. That moment passed quickly. Once again I could hear Anita's voice. She was asking us to call on the angel and see if we could get a name. All of sudden, I saw before me the vision of a beautiful angelic being. She wore a long white robe with a gold string around the waist. Her golden yellow curls covered her shoulders. Her face was radiant. Her eyes were luminous, and she had the most joyful smile.

"My name is Lily, and I am the one that helped Chantal cross over." She was so stunning I was speechless. I started to sob, I felt such peace. It was such a profound comfort for me to know that this beautiful angelic being was with my daughter at the time of her passing. "I thank you from the bottom of my heart for being there." I saw Lily for only a split second, but during that short time I knew why. That was her gift and message to me.

I couldn't move. I was frozen in my seat. I just sat there and enjoyed that special moment. At the end of the meditation, we all shared what we had seen, and that is when everyone in the room said they felt Chantal's presence. There was one lady in particular who said she had never felt the presence of a spirit before this night, but she felt my daughter. I can't begin to tell you what a wonderful experience this was, especially because Chantal made her presence known so soon after her death. I was so grateful to Anita for having this class in honour of my beautiful daughter.

On Wednesday we needed to go back to London to pick up Chantal's remains. Thomas had asked to come with us. After breakfast, my husband happened to look at his cell phone. It said he had one missed call. When he looked to see who it was from, it said there was one missed call from Chantal's cell phone, Tuesday, July 24, at 11:46 p.m. We could not believe it. We started to cry. I had my daughter's cell phone, but it was not even on. She passed away on July 22. This message came from Chantal on her phone two days later.

Chantal left this on Alain's phone to let us know she was with us at the meditation class, and she is around us now. I told her how much I loved her, missed her, and thanked her for being there. This is a picture taken of my husband's cell phone with the message from Chantal's cell.

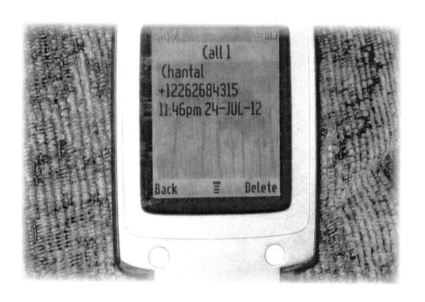

We picked Thomas up around nine that morning. It was pretty quiet in the car on the way there. Everything was ready for us. All I had to do was sign some papers. When it was time to leave the office, my son voluntarily picked up the urn. That was a very touching moment for me; I felt very proud of him. On the way home Chantal sat in the back seat with her big brother, Thomas.

That night I had a vivid dream. I heard our front door bell ring. I pulled the covers off me and almost got up to answer the door, but then I heard, *Don't get up. It's me, Mom, at the door. Just want you to know I am around.* I pulled the covers over me and went back to sleep. This too was a sign from her.

Whenever I feel heartbroken over the loss of my daughter, I talk to her. I tell her how much I love her, miss her, and long to hold her. Many times Chantal makes her presence known to me. I start to cry, and within a few minutes I feel a sense of peace, comfort, and love. What a wonderful gift my beautiful daughter brings me.

Chantal has brought me several messages from other mediums, through friends and my students telling me how much she loves me and how proud she is. I teach mediumship classes, and when my daughter comes through, bringing them a message to give to me, I call her "teacher's little helper." These messages bring me such pleasure and contentment.

The arrangements were made for Chantal's service, and all we had to do was to wait for those who were coming from out of town to arrive. The service would be on Monday, the week after her death. All that week I felt as though I were on a high dose of adrenaline, making sure all the preparations were taken care of. Now reality was setting in. I was getting dressed to go when it hit me. *Oh, my God! I am getting ready for my daughter's funeral.* I had a sick feeling in the pit of my stomach. I would not have wished this feeling and this moment on my worst enemy.

My spiritual training helps me to understand why we come here and why we choose to leave, but it did not make it easier to realize that my daughter was no longer here in physical form where I could hold her next to me. I felt empty inside, as though a part of me had been taken away. I prayed to God to give me the strength to make it through the day.

We arrived at the funeral home an hour before the service, and the parking lot was already filling up. As we entered the room, my eyes immediately turned to Chantal's picture, with her radiant smile and bright shining eyes. It seemed to fill the room with her presence. I felt she was giving me the courage and knowledge that everything was going to be okay. Her urn was surrounded by beautiful flowers, two angel statues, and pictures of her at all ages.

I had asked my niece Jennifer to download four of Chantal's favourite songs to play at her memorial. The first song we played before Reverend Anita started the service was "Live like You Were Dying" by Tim McGraw. I had no idea my daughter listened to country music. This song was so appropriate. Chantal did live her life to the fullest, as though it were her last. To this day I listen to this song. I cry every time I hear it, but they are good tears.

Chantal's aunt Ginette got up and talked about the wonderful woman Chantal grew up to become, how brave she was throughout her illnesses. Alissa talked about the special friendship the two of them had, the love Chantal felt towards her family and how much we meant to her. Adam made us all laugh when he told us how hard he had to work to get Chantal to go out with him in the beginning, and what a loving and caring person she was. Jeremy talked about Chantal's courage and what a great friend she was, how happy he was to have known her and what an inspiration she was to so many people. A few other friends spoke about their friendship with Chantal and shared some of their stories.

I was the last to speak. I wasn't sure if I would be able to get up in front of all those people during this sad time, but God gave me the strength to do it. I would like to share with you what I said.

Dearest Daughter,

Oh, my sweet baby! You had no idea how much of an impact you left on people you came into contact with. Your beautiful smile always radiated. Your compassion and love was felt by everyone. You were a true gift from God, and you are a wonderful spirit that will live on. Although you left this earth at a young age, I am truly grateful to have had you in my life for twenty-nine wonderful years. Throughout all your illnesses, you always showed your strength to fight, and that gave me the strength to cope. I already feel your presence and know you will always be around us, and that gives me great comfort. I love you with all my heart, I will miss you, but you will never, ever be forgotten. With that, dear God, I release her back to you with peace in my heart.

Love, Mom

The service lasted about forty-five minutes. My brother-in-law Tom told me later he did not see too many dry eyes in the room. My sister's husband, Sandy, told her people were lined up outside all the way to the parking lot. There were over three hundred people that day that came to pay their respects to Chantal. My friend Reverend Anita had a beautiful service for a beautiful soul. I was so grateful. I will never forget it.

To this day my daughter Chantal continues to communicate from the other side. She sends messages and makes her presence known to my husband and me, to friends and certain family members. I felt inspired by my daughter to write this book, to help parents whose children have been diagnosed with cancer or heart disease or are grieving the loss of their child.

When you first hear the diagnosis, you are devastated, and you feel helpless. You know that your life and your child's life will be changed forever. But it doesn't mean his or her life is over. My daughter lived cancer-free for twenty-five years and lived a good fifteen years with heart disease. You need to have faith and believe your child will get better.

When someone dies at a young age, you often hear people say, "Oh, what a shame they died so young. They didn't have a chance to live life, have children, or grow old." I have also heard the expression, "How could God take them at such a young age?" My daughter lived to be twenty-nine years old. In those short years, she lived her life to the fullest. God did not take her; it was her time to go.

My daughter's life was never easy. Chantal suffered much pain throughout her lifetime. Yet her strong will and determination allowed her to give herself another chance at life. That takes courage. I don't know that I would have gone through such pain. Even though my daughter did not survive, I kept my faith and trust in God.

Every one of us has come here to experience life for God. So, like all of us, Chantal had a reason and a purpose to be here. This was to accomplish what she set out to achieve. Chantal did exactly that. She touched countless hearts. Her loving, caring, and compassionate personality changed the lives of many people, including mine. Her courage and strong will enabled her to live life fearlessly.

She always thought of others, even at the time of her death. By donating her corneas and tissues, my beautiful daughter was able to give a three-year-old little girl and an older person the gift of sight.

Months after Chantal's passing I was preparing for a client's reading. As I was meditating I felt the presence of my daughter's spirit beside me. Whenever I feel Chantal around me, I get very emotional. I was quite surprised and not sure why she made her presence known to me at that particular time; however, I was not about to question it. I always feel such comfort when she is around me. Her exact words were, *Mom, I am so sorry you are in pain, but I no longer wanted to be in pain.* Chantal felt she needed to apologize for causing me such sorrow.

After hearing those words I started sobbing. Once I was able to compose myself, I said to her, "Honey, it is okay. I understand. I didn't want you suffering anymore. I know you did all you could." When a loved one is dying, we want to hang on to them for our own selfish reasons. As heartbreaking as it is, we must let them go. The fact that they are no longer suffering should bring us comfort. I know it has for me.

I believe that your deceased child in the spirit world hears your thoughts and feels your love, your pain, and your agony. They want to help and guide us even from the other side. We must talk to them as though they were here. We must be aware of their signs and, most of all, be open to receiving their powerful healing messages. They often come through by means of electronics, such as radio, computers, and lights flicking on and off. They may leave a certain odor in the air, something that reminds you of them. I know my dad is around me when I smell his pipe tobacco. They are also known to leave coins or feathers around.

Losing my child has been difficult for me, but what helps me in my sorrow is to know and understand that even though she is no longer here in physical form, her soul lives on. She can still communicate and bring me messages from the other side. I have my moments. But knowing that my daughter is around me is the best gift that I could ever allow myself to receive.

Chantal's life had great meaning. I do not look at her life as over. I look at her passing as a new beginning. She came on earth to experience life for a short time. She had a reason and a purpose to come here, and I know in my heart she was able to accomplish what she came to do. She taught me to be more loving, more caring, and more compassionate towards others. These wonderful qualities we should all possess, to help us learn and grow spiritually. She is always in my thoughts, and I get great comfort knowing she is around me, guiding me. My love for her grows stronger every day.

Coping with a Child's Serious Illness

A *Daughter's Journey* was written to help families whose child is diagnosed with cancer or heart disease and also to help them during their time of grief. Every person reacts in a different way, but the fears and the emotions are pretty well the same for all of us.

It is very important that you listen to your child when he or she complains of a pain. Don't wait. Have it checked out right away.

The first stage after receiving the news is denial. You may say to yourself, *This can't be true. This is not happening to us. They must have made a mistake.* You want this horrible nightmare to go away.

Then the fear steps in, and all the emotions that come over you cannot be described. It is so devastating; it makes you feel helpless, angry, and afraid of the unknown. You want to blame someone. You feel you have lost control.

This does not mean that your child was given a death sentence. Chantal lived cancer-free for twenty-five wonderful years, and fifteen good years with heart disease.

Listen to everything the doctors have to say. Ask them to repeat it if you do not understand. Never be afraid to ask questions. Keep a journal, and, if necessary, get a second opinion.

Be patient, compassionate, and loving towards your child when he or she takes fear and frustration out on you. Remember it is very scary for the child, and this is the time he or she needs your support the most.

An illness can create a lot of stress in our lives. It can make your relationship stronger, or it can destroy it.

It is necessary to have an open communication with every member of your family during this difficult time. Be honest and do not be afraid to express your true feelings.

This is a family disease. Never take it for granted that the other members of the family, especially the siblings, understand what is going on. Talk to them. Allow them to express their feelings about what is happening. They need to be involved in the care of their sibling, so be sure to keep them updated with all the developments.

Attending group counselling is very important to everyone concerned. It allows you to share all your feelings with other families who are experiencing the same emotions.

Your lives will certainly change, and you will have to make many adjustments. My rock through the hard years was my faith and trust that God would take care of all of us, and he did.

Recommended Books

These powerful books helped me during my time of change.

You Can Heal Your Life and *The Power Is Within You* by Louise Hay

Dying to Be Me by Anita Moorjani

The Game of Life and How to Play It by Florence Scovel Shinn

The Power of Your Subconscious Mind by Dr. Joseph Murphy

The Power of Now and *A New Earth Awakening to Your Life's Purpose* by Eckhart Tolle

As a Man Thinketh by James Allen

Letting Go by Guy Finley

Sylvia Browne Books, which are too many to list

Destiny of Souls and *Journey of Souls* by Michael Newton

Communication with God, a trilogy by Neale Donald Walsch

The Secret by Rhonda Byrne

Healing Grief and *Talking to Heaven* by James van Praagh

Change Your Thoughts—Change Your Life and *The Shift Movie* by Wayne Dyer

The Healing Codes by Dr. Alex Loyd

Healing with the Angels, Divine Guidance, and *Daily Guidance from Your Angels* by Doreen Virtue

Remember the Future and *The Map* by Collette Barron Reid

About the Author

Louise Michaud is an ordained spiritualist minister, medium, healer, teacher and spiritual counsellor. Born in Quebec City, she was three years old when her family moved to St. Catharines, Canada. She still happily resides there with her husband, Alain, plus her two cats, Oliver and Spencer. Louise received her training and ordination at the Fellowships of the Spirit, School of Spiritual Healing and Prophecy, in the town of Lily Dale, New York. There she was able to enhance her natural psychic-mediumistic abilities. Lily Dale is a community established in 1879 and is noted as the world's largest centre for spiritual development.

Louise has attended workshops with the world-renowned psychic Sylvia Browne, medium Colette Baron Reid, Doreen Virtue, and Neale Donald Walsch, author of the *Communication with God* books. She is certified as an ACP, angel practitioner (communicating with the angelic realm). Louise has a flourishing private healing and reading practice. She teaches mediumship classes and on occasion serves as assistant minister at East Hamilton Spiritual Church.

For more information about Louise, please visit her website:
www.messagefromspirits.com

~ *NOTES* ~

~ *NOTES* ~

~ *NOTES* ~

~ *NOTES* ~

CPSIA information can be obtained at www.ICGtesting.com
Printed in the USA
BVOW07s2316051014

369454BV00002B/2/P